Seasonal Distribution and Aerial Surveys of Mountain Goats in Mount Rainier, North Cascades, and Olympic National Parks, Washington

By Kurt Jenkins, U.S. Geological Survey; Katherine Beirne, Patricia Happe, and Roger Hoffman, Olympic National Park; Cliff Rice, Washington Department of Fish and Wildlife; and Jim Schaberl, Mount Rainier National Park

Prepared in cooperation with the U.S. National Park Service and Washington Department of Fish and Wildlife

Open-File Report 2011–1107

U.S. Department of the Interior
U.S. Geological Survey

U.S. Department of the Interior
KEN SALAZAR, Secretary

U.S. Geological Survey
Marcia K. McNutt, Director

U.S. Geological Survey, Reston, Virginia: 2011

For more information on the USGS—the Federal source for science about the Earth,
its natural and living resources, natural hazards, and the environment,
visit http://www.usgs.gov or call 1–888–ASK–USGS.

For an overview of USGS information products, including maps, imagery, and publications,
visit http://www.usgs.gov/pubprod

To order this and other USGS information products, visit http://store.usgs.gov

Suggested citation:
Jenkins, Kurt, Beirne, Katherine, Happe, Patricia, Hoffman, Roger, Rice, Cliff, and Schaberl, Jim, 2011, Seasonal
distribution and aerial surveys of mountain goats in Mount Rainier, North Cascades, and Olympic National Parks,
Washington: U.S. Geological Survey Open-File Report 2011-1107, 56 p.

Contents

Figures

Tables

Conversion Factors

Inch/Pound to SI

Multiply	By	To obtain
foot (ft)	0.3048	meter (m)

SI to Inch/Pound

Multiply	By	To obtain
meter (m)	3.281	foot (ft)
kilometer (km)	0.6214	mile (mi)
hectare (ha)	2.471	acre
square kilometer (km^2)	247.1	acre
milligram (g)	0.00003527	ounce, avoirdupois (oz)

Temperature in degrees Celsius (°C) may be converted to degrees Fahrenheit (°F) as follows:

$$°F=(1.8×°C)+32.$$

Seasonal Distribution and Aerial Surveys of Mountain Goats in Mount Rainier, North Cascades, and Olympic National Parks, Washington

By Kurt Jenkins[1], Katherine Beirne[2], Patricia Happe[2], Roger Hoffman[2], Cliff Rice[3], and Jim Schaberl[4,5]

Abstract

We described the seasonal distribution of Geographic Positioning System (GPS)-collared mountain goats (*Oreamnos americanus*) in Mount Rainier, North Cascades, and Olympic National Parks to evaluate aerial survey sampling designs and provide general information for park managers. This work complemented a companion study published elsewhere of aerial detection biases of mountain goat surveys in western Washington. Specific objectives reported here were to determine seasonal and altitudinal movements, home range distributions, and temporal dynamics of mountain goat movements in and out of aerial survey sampling frames established within each park. We captured 25 mountain goats in Mount Rainier (9), North Cascades (5), and Olympic (11) National Parks, and fitted them with GPS-collars programmed to obtain 6–8 locations daily. We obtained location data on 23 mountain goats for a range of 39–751 days from 2003 to 2008. Altitudinal distributions of GPS-collared mountain goats varied individually and seasonally, but median altitudes used by individual goats during winter ranged from 817 to 1,541 meters in Olympic and North Cascades National Parks, and 1,215 to 1,787 meters in Mount Rainier National Park. Median altitudes used by GPS-collared goats during summer ranged from 1,312 to 1,819 meters in Olympic and North Cascades National Parks, and 1,780 to 2,061 meters in Mount Rainier National Park. GPS-collared mountain goats generally moved from low-altitude winter ranges to high-altitude summer ranges between June 11 and June 19 (range April 24–July 3) and from summer to winter ranges between October 26 and November 9 (range September 11–December 23). Seasonal home ranges (95 percent of adaptive kernel utilization distribution) of males and female mountain goats were highly variable, ranging from 1.6 to 37.0 kilometers during summers and 0.7 to 9.5 kilometers during winters. Locations of GPS-collared mountain goats were almost 100 percent within the sampling frame used for mountain goat surveys in Mount Rainier National Park, whereas generally greater than 80 and greater than 60 percent of locations were within sampling units delineated in North Cascades and Olympic National Parks, respectively. Presence of GPS-collared mountain goats within the sampling frame of Olympic National Park varied by diurnal period (midday versus crepuscular), survey season (July versus September), and the interaction of diurnal period and survey season. Aerial surveys conducted in developing a sightability model for mountain goat aerial surveys indicated mean detection probabilities of 0.69, 0.76, and 0.87 in North Cascades, Olympic, and Mount Rainier National Parks, respectively. Higher detection probabilities in Mount Rainier likely reflected larger group sizes and more open habitat conditions than in North Cascades and Olympic National Parks. Use of sightability models will reduce biases of population estimates in each park, but resulting population estimates must still be considered minimum population estimates in Olympic and North Cascades National Parks because the current sampling frames do not encompass those populations completely. Because mountain goats were reliably present within the sampling frame in Mount Rainier National Park, we found no compelling need to adjust mountain goat survey boundaries in that park. Expanding survey coverage in North Cascades and Olympic National Parks to more reliably encompass the altitudinal distribution of mountain goats during summer would enhance population estimation accuracy in the future. Lowering the altitude boundary of mountain goat survey units by as little as 100 meters to 1,425 meters in Olympic National Park would increase mountain goat presence within the survey and reduce variation in counts related to movements of mountain goats outside the survey boundaries.

[1]U.S. Geological Survey, Forest and Rangeland Ecosystem Science Center, 600 E. Park Avenue, Port Angeles, WA 98362.

[2]Olympic National Park, 600 E. Park Avenue, Port Angeles, WA 98362

[3]Wildlife Program, Washington Department of Fish and Wildlife, 600 Capitol Way N., Olympia WA 98501

[4]Mount Rainier National Park, 55210 238th Ave E., Ashford, WA 98304

[5]Current Address: Shenandoah National Park, 3655 U.S. Highway 211 E., Luray, VA 22835

Introduction

Managing populations of mountain goats in Washington's Cascades Range and Olympic Mountains requires reliable estimates of population size. Accurate population estimates are needed to establish harvest limits for mountain goats in the Cascades Range, where local populations have declined in recent decades (Rice and Gay, 2010), and to monitor their conservation status in Mount Rainier and North Cascades National Parks. In the Olympic Mountains, where mountain goats were introduced into Olympic National Park in the 1920s and populations expanded over several decades, populations are monitored to identify risks of ecosystem degradation associated with population growth of this non-native species in a national park (Houston and others, 1986, 1991, 1994a).

In 2005, the U.S. Geological Survey (USGS) and National Park Service (NPS) joined efforts with Washington Department of Fish and Wildlife (WDFW) to estimate detection biases and improve accuracy of helicopter surveys of mountain goats in western Washington. The correction for detection bias is necessary because not all animals present are observed and counted during aerial surveys, resulting in the underestimation of actual numbers of animals present (Samuel and others, 1987; Gonzalez-Voyer and others, 2001; Udevitz and others, 2006). Other partners participating in the estimation of visibility biases of mountain goat aerial surveys included the U.S. Forest Service, Sauk-Suiattle Tribe, and Western Washington University. We completed that project in 2009 with the publication of a sightability model designed to improve the accuracy of aerial surveys of mountain goats throughout western Washington (Rice and others, 2009).

USGS and NPS participation in this study was motivated by controversy surrounding a former NPS proposal to control non-native populations of mountain goats in Olympic National Park through culling (National Park Service, 1995). A Congressionally mandated review of the scientific information on mountain goats in Olympic National Park focused on estimation methods used to track population trends. Early studies in Olympic National Park indicated aerial surveys accounted for approximately 66 percent of the population (Houston and others, 1986), based on the index manipulation method first described by Caughley (1977). Consequently, raw counts obtained from aerial surveys of mountain goats in Olympic National Park were increased by a factor of 1.52 (that is, 1/0.66) in subsequent surveys to account for the unobserved population fraction (Houston and others, 1986, 1991, 1994a).

The independent review team commended the overall design and execution of mountain goat surveys in Olympic National Park, but described the reliance of the 66 percent efficiency factor as the weak link in the estimation process (Noss and others, 2000) because observational biases are not static and may change as population abundance or environmental conditions vary over time (Noss and others, 2000).

Our previous work revealed that detection probabilities of mountain goats generally averaged from 75 to 91 percent in different populations throughout western Washington, but also varied among individual groups of mountain goats reflecting differences in group size and habitat characteristics (Rice and others, 2009). We also determined that 11 GPS-collared mountain goats were outside the established survey areas during surveys conducted in developing these sightability models, indicating that movements of GPS-collared mountain goats outside the survey areas may present an unmeasured source of bias in population estimates. Others have suggested that if a significant or varying segment of a surveyed population is 'unavailable' to the survey, then it may be useful to separate and estimate two components of bias—one related to the failure to see all animals present, and another related to the segment of population unavailable to the survey (Pollock and others, 2004).

The purpose of this report is to describe seasonal distribution patterns of GPS-collared mountain goats within Mount Rainier, North Cascades, and Olympic National Parks. This work addresses the following questions regarding the current aerial surveys used to estimate population size and trends of mountain goats: Do mountain goats spend appreciable time outside the survey areas during summer? Do mountain goats move in and out of the survey areas seasonally or diurnally? Answers to such questions are needed to determine whether survey units should be redrawn to better represent habitats occupied by the populations of interest. Descriptive information provided on seasonal and diurnal movements of mountain goats will also be useful for interpreting mountain goat biology and natural history to park visitors and informing park planning decisions.

Our specific objectives were to determine the seasonal altitudinal movements of mountain goats in the three parks, and determine the seasonal and diurnal use of the aerial survey sampling areas established within each. We also provide descriptive information on the seasonal range shifts and home ranges used by GPS-collared mountain goats and report the raw data from aerial surveys associated with sightability model development in each park. Those descriptions and data are provided primarily for park management and archival purposes.

Study Area

Our study area included seasonal ranges of mountain goats in and adjacent to three mountainous wilderness parks in western Washington: Mount Rainier and North Cascades National Parks in the Cascades Range and Olympic National Park in the Olympic Mountains, which form the mountainous core of the Olympic Peninsula (fig. 1). Mountain goats typically inhabited altitudes ranging from approximately 800 to 2,000 m in the Cascades Range and 800 to 1,700 m in the Olympic Range, spanning a wide range of habitats that included montane forests, subalpine parklands, alpine tundra, rock and snow (Stevens, 1979; Rice, 2008). Montane forests primarily were representative of the Western Hemlock (*Tsuga heterophylla*), Pacific Silver Fir (*Abies amabilis*), and Mountain Hemlock (*Tsuga mertensiana*) forest zones of western Washington (Franklin and Dyrness, 1988). Timberline is highly variable among the three parks but generally averaged approximately 1,450 m in the central Olympic Mountains and North Cascades and approximately 1,600 m in Mount Rainier and the eastern Olympic Range. In each park, a broad zone of subalpine parklands and subalpine meadows formed a dynamic ecotone between the upper edge of tree dominance and increasingly harsh alpine environments at higher altitudes (Franklin and Dyrness, 1988). Subalpine parklands comprised mosaics of subalpine fir (*Abies lasiocarpa*) and mountain hemlock forests, and a variety of heath-shrub, sedge (*Carex* spp.), grass, and forb-dominated meadow communities depending on local variations in soil development, moisture, winter snow depth, and growing season (Fonda and Bliss, 1969; Kuramoto and Bliss, 1970; Henderson, 1973). The alpine zone, generally at altitudes above 1,800 m, consists of very steep and rugged assortments of alpine tundra communities, bare rock, talus, scree, glaciers, and snowfields (Bliss, 1969; Hamann, 1972, both summarized in Franklin and Dyrness, 1988).

Methods

We captured mountain goats using a variety of methods and personnel. From 2003 to 2007, WDFW and NPS personnel captured several goats in and around Mount Rainier and North Cascades National Parks, through either aerial or ground-based darting (Rice and others, 2009). During summers of 2005 and 2007, we captured three goats through leg-noosing and physical restraint (Stevens, 1979; Olson, 1994). Most mountain goats collared in the three parks were captured by an independent crew on contract with the Department of the Interior for animal capture operations (Leading Edge Aviation, Lewiston, Idaho). The contract team captured 17 mountain goats from September 18–21, 2005, through aerial darting with 2.4 mg carfentanil citrate (appendix 1). Capture procedures were approved by the Animal Care and Use Committee at the Large Animal Research Center at Oregon State University.

Crews fitted each captured mountain goat with a GPS tracking collar (Vectronic™ GPS Plus-4. Vectronic Aerospace, Berlin, Germany). All collars were color coded to facilitate individual recognition during aerial surveys. Each collar contained a 12-channel GPS receiver, very-high frequency (VHF) beacon, an ultra-high frequency beacon, data storage memory, and a radio-modem for remote transfer of data to and from the collar. We programmed each of the collars to attempt to obtain location fixes every 3–4 hours (varying between animals). Most animals captured by WDFW personnel were fitted with collars programmed for location fixes every 3 hours, whereas animals captured by contracted crews from Olympic National Park and the USGS were fitted with collars programmed to obtain location fixes every 4 hours.

Seasonal Distribution

We remotely downloaded location data stored on board each GPS-collar at approximately 3-month intervals from September 2005 to September 2007. Additionally, Cliff Rice (Washington Department of Fish and Wildlife) made available the downloaded data files for mountain goats that were previously collared within or near Mount Rainier and North Cascades National Parks, and whose home ranges broadly overlapped those park lands. We collared one mountain goat late in the study in Olympic National Park and obtained data on its movements until late summer 2008. Hence, the analysis of mountain goat distribution was based on data collected from 2003 to 2007 in Mount Rainier and North Cascades National Parks and 2005 to 2008 in Olympic National Park.

Typically, we downloaded location data remotely through UHF radio communications using a Vectronic™ handheld terminal operated from a fixed-wing aircraft. Frequently, we also downloaded data from a helicopter immediately following an aerial survey. To guard against using faulty or erroneous location data in subsequent analyses, we removed data outliers by screening for invalid dates associated with faulty data. We also examined 55 data outliers that lay beyond the interquartile ranges measured from the median x and y coordinates of each mountain goat. We retained questionable outliers if there were other locations in the same general area that either preceded or followed the questionable locations chronologically. We deleted less than 10 questionable outliers that had no supportive locations nearby. We determined altitudes of all fixes from a 10-m digital elevation model using ArcGIS 9.1.

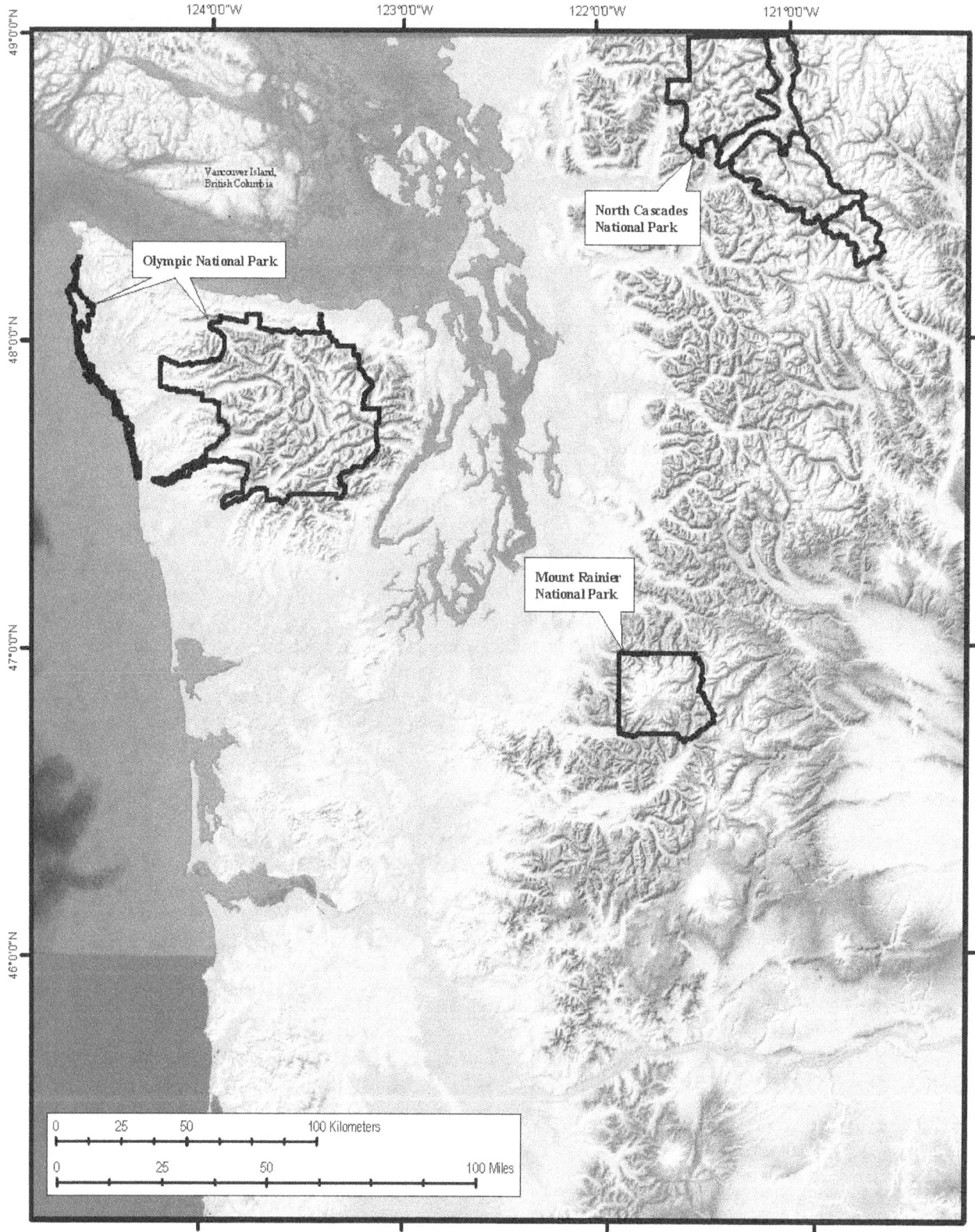

Figure 1.   Locations of Mount Rainier and North Cascades National Parks in the Cascades Range and Olympic National Park on the Olympic Peninsula, Washington.

Location data obtained from GPS telemetry collars may be biased by variations in GPS reception in different habitats or from animals in different activities (for example, resting versus standing) (Sager-Fradkin and others, 2007; Schwartz and others, 2009). Modeling approaches used previously to adjust GPS location data for GPS bias have met only limited success (D'Eon, 2003; Sager-Fradkin and others, 2007). Hence, we did not adjust location data based on detection biases of GPS telemetry in different environments. We expect GPS telemetry, however, to under-represent use of low-altitude forested habitats where GPS reception typically is most obstructed (Wells, 2006).

Altitudinal Movements

We described seasonal altitudinal movements of collared goats by computing and graphically displaying the mean (±SE) altitudes used by collared goats during each week of each year. Because seasonal altitudinal movements of mountain goats were highly individualistic, we estimated calendar dates for individual mountain goats that best corresponded with seasonal transitions between summer and winter ranges. Based on methods described by Rice (2008), we used the non-parametric Van der Waerden test statistic (Conover, 1980) to contrast the magnitude of altitudinal separation for iteratively selected potential start and end dates of summer and winter seasons. We identified the starting dates of summer and winter range use as the date that produced the largest seasonal separation in altitudes used by each mountain goat based on the Van der Waerden test statistic. Because the statistic was used only as an index of separation to identify timing of distributional shifts, we did not evaluate statistical significance of the seasonal separations in altitude.

Use of Mountain Goat Survey Areas During Summer

We used a graphical approach to describe diurnal use of the aerial survey sampling areas by mountain goats. The sampling area is described further below, but consisted of the collective set of survey units that comprised the sampling frame developed for mountain goat surveys in each park. Each GPS telemetry location was labeled as occurring either within the survey sampling frame, indicating that the animal would be available to be seen in an aerial survey, or outside the sampling frame, indicating the animal was not available to the survey. We graphed the mean (±SE) altitudes used by collared goats during selected hours of the 24-hour cycle and the mean percentages of GPS locations that occurred within the

mountain goat survey frame. To minimize seasonal influences and because aerial surveys generally are flown during the last 3 weeks of July, we limited those graphical summaries to include only data obtained between July 10 and July 31 each year. To guard against potential effects of aircraft responses, we did not use data corresponding to days that goats were surveyed from a helicopter.

We used logistic regression to model the influence of diurnal period, ambient temperature, and survey season on the probability that mountain goats were present within the sampling frame in Olympic National Park (Hosmer and Lemeshow, 2000). We did not model goat presence within sampling frames of Mount Rainier National Park because the collared mountain goats were nearly always present, nor within North Cascades National Park because of small sample sizes. We hypothesized *apriori* that mountain goats in Olympic National Park may be less frequently present in the sampling frame during hot weather or during the midday based on previous speculation that mountain goats may descend in altitude during hot weather (Houston and others, 1986, 1994b). We also speculated that mountain goat presence within the sampling frame may vary from summer to early autumn in response to changing forage phenology, food habits, or thermal regime. We modeled the presence of a collared goat in the sampling frame as a binary dependent variable (0 for animals not present versus 1 for animals present). We examined effects of the following predictors: a binary variable for crepuscular (5:00–9:00 and 17:00–21:00) versus midday (9:01–16:59) time periods, mean ambient temperature of the survey day (°C), and a binary variable delineating two survey seasons corresponding with the last 3 weeks of July and September, respectively. We chose these two potential seasonal survey periods because mountain goats generally are surveyed in Olympic National Park during the last 3 weeks in July, but September also has been used and is a plausible alternative. August was not considered a feasible alternative for mountain goat surveys due to peak human visitation of the park's backcountry and because hot weather in August typically poses logistical difficulties for conducting aerial surveys from helicopters at high altitudes.

We used Akaike's Information Criterion (AIC), Akaike differences (ΔAIC), and Akaike weights (w) to identify the most parsimonious model of mountain goat presence within the sampling frame (Burnham and Anderson, 2002). We calculated the variance inflation factor, $\hat{c}$ (Pearson's x^2/df) to evaluate model fit and determine whether to apply a quasi-likelihood variance expansion term for over dispersed data (if $\hat{c}$ was substantially greater than 1; Burnham and Anderson, 2002). We performed these statistical analyses using SAS 8.2 software (SAS Institute, Cary, NC).

Home Range Utilization Distributions

To provide descriptive information to park managers on the distributions of individual mountain goats, we described seasonal home ranges and core areas using the 95, 80, and 50 percent adaptive kernel estimators, respectively (Worton, 1989). We used likelihood cross-validation (LCV) computed in Program Animal Space Use 1.2 (available at http://www.cnr.uidaho.edu/population_ecology/animal_space_use.htm) for choosing the optimal smoothing parameter (Horne and Garton, 2006). We chose LCV over the more commonly used Least-Squares Cross Validation because it is more robust to clustered data, less prone to undersmoothing problems, and because we sought a conservative approach to potential autocorrelation among GPS-locations (Horne and Garton, 2006). We plugged the LCV smoothing parameter into Home Range Tools for ARCGIS to compute adaptive kernel home range and core area estimates (Rodgers and others, 2005), based on 95, 80, and 50 percent contours of the utilization distribution. All seasonal ranges are based on the delineations of summer and winter range use periods described above.

Aerial Surveys

We conducted sightability trials as the basis for developing aerial sightability models for mountain goats (Rice and others, 2009). Each attempt of an aerial survey crew to detect a known group of mountain goats was considered an independent sightability trial. Locations of known groups were determined primarily through GPS-telemetry of the collared mountain goats before the surveys, but occasionally we conducted sightability trials based on mountain goats whose locations were determined opportunistically by independent ground observers. Details of methods used to conduct sightability trials were provided by Rice and others (2009).

Our priority was to obtain as many sightability trials as possible, so we focused surveys in areas known to contain GPS-collared mountain goats. Because we did not survey entire populations or sample populations probabilistically, we cannot estimate park-wide abundance of mountain goats from the sightability trials conducted. Here, we report survey results from selected survey units as a source for future reference in comparing counts within specific units.

We divided each of the parks into approximately 500-ha aerial survey polygons or sampling units (median=472 ha, interquartile range=240–545 ha). Because each park had a different history in conducting surveys and used different methods to delineate aerial survey areas, we did not use a consistent definition of the sampling areas among parks. In Olympic National Park, we used survey polygons used since

1983 for park-wide monitoring of mountain goats (Houston and others, 1984, 1991; fig. 2). In Olympic National Park, the sampling frame was limited to habitat above 1,520 m (about 5,000 ft) excluding glaciers. In Mount Rainier National Park, the sampling frame was drawn to include all high-altitude habitats considered subjectively as suitable mountain goat habitat (that is, there was no fixed lower altitude limit to the sampling frame) (fig. 3). In North Cascades National Park, survey boundaries also included all likely mountain goat habitats (fig. 4). To improve efficiency of the sightability trial surveys in North Cascades National Park, we truncated surveys at a lower altitude limit of 1,220 m (about 4,000 ft) (fig. 4).

In each park, we completed two aerial surveys of polygons known to have GPS-collared mountain goats present during summers 2006–07, once each during July 10–18 and July 24–August 2. In Olympic National Park, we completed an additional survey during September 2007 to make up for inclement weather that prevented us from completing the July surveys. Prior to each survey (generally 1–7 days), one of us that was not participating in the upcoming survey radio-tracked each of the GPS-collared mountain goats from a fixed-wing airplane, downloaded all location data from each goat, plotted recent movements, and selected survey polygons that were likely to contain GPS-collared mountain goats. To create uncertainty in where survey crews might expect to find collared mountain goats, we selected 2–3 survey polygons for every collared animal. In addition, we sent ground survey crews opportunistically to selected units to locate additional groups of unmarked mountain goats and observe them during aerial surveys as a means to increase the sample of sightability trials.

Due to extremely irregular topography of mountain goat habitats, it was not possible to strictly standardize survey flight coverage of each of the sampled units. Adherence to standardized flight paths or flight speeds would not allow all suitable habitats to be searched effectively. Instead, we specified that each survey unit should be examined with multiple survey passes flown at an altitude of about 150–200 m above terrain, on contours 100–300 m apart, and airspeeds averaging between 65 and 110 km/hr as needed to ensure safe and complete area coverage. All surveys reported here were conducted from a Bell Jet Ranger or Hughes 500MD helicopter. Survey teams consisted of the pilot, a primary observer seated beside the pilot, a secondary observer in the back seat behind the primary observer and a navigator behind the pilot. During surveys, primary and secondary observers were nearly always on the side of the helicopter facing terrain. Additional description of aerial surveys is provided by Rice and others (2009).

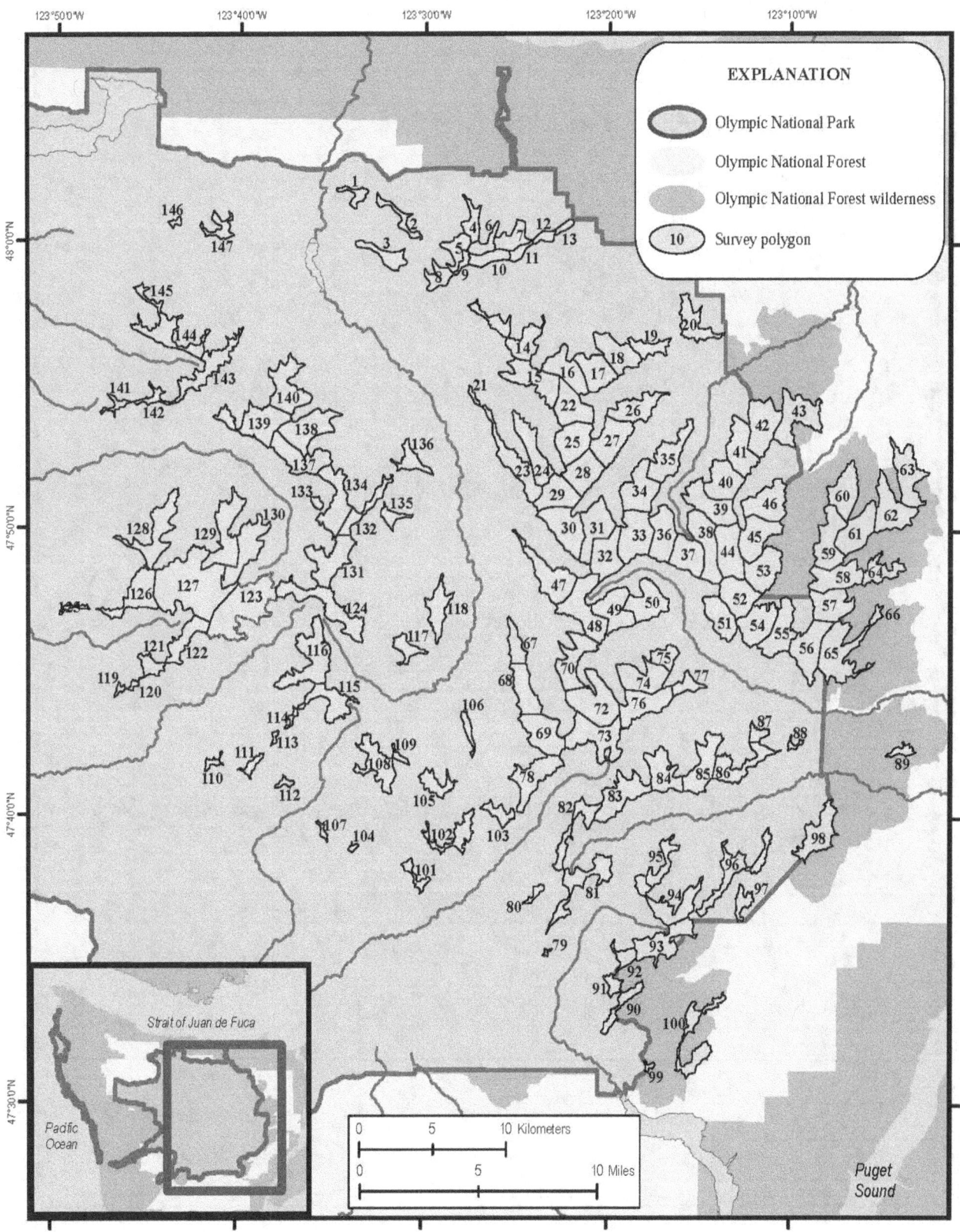

Figure 2. Aerial survey polygons comprising the sampling frame used for aerial surveys of mountain goats in Olympic National Park, Washington.

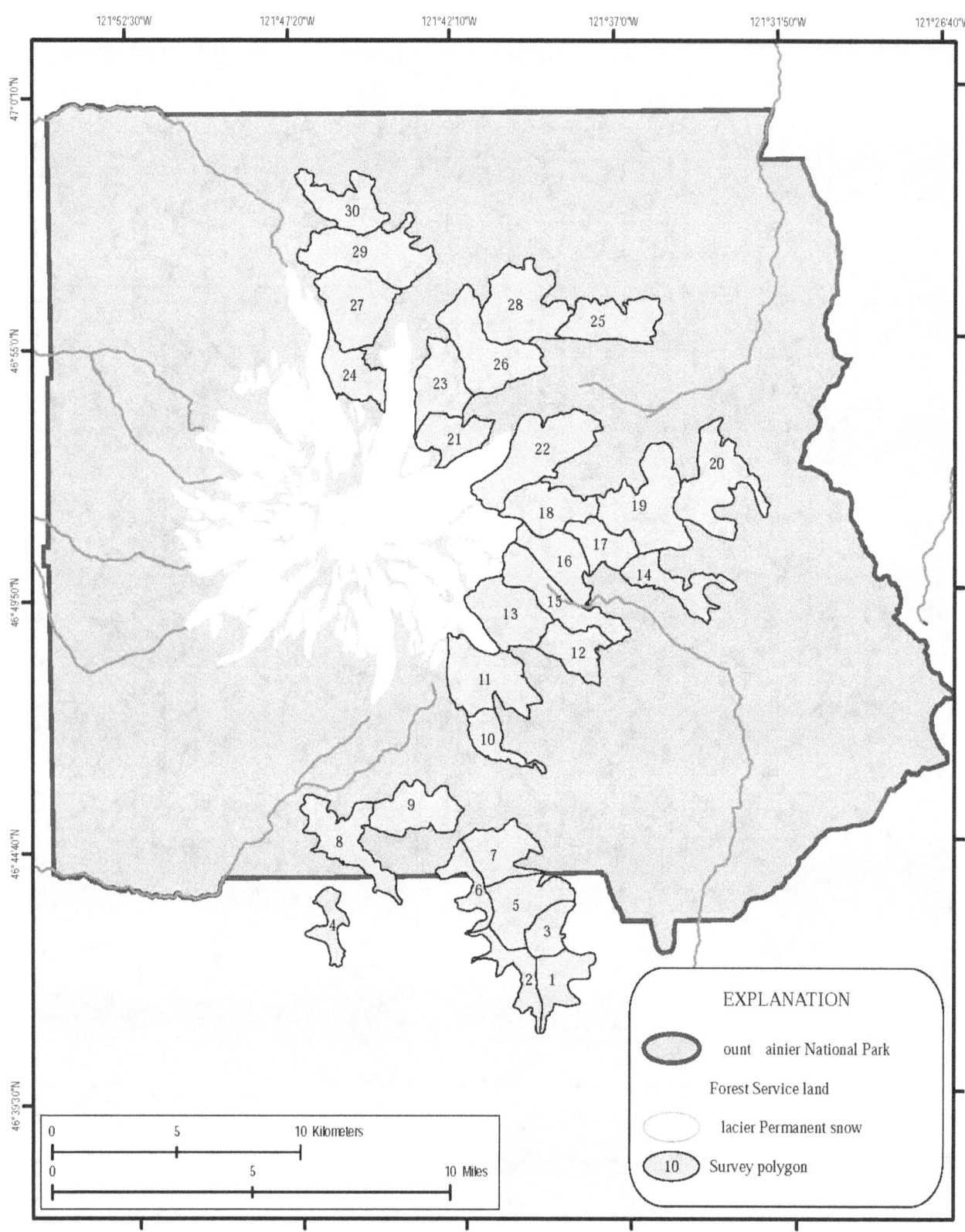

Figure 3.   Aerial survey polygons comprising the sampling frame used for aerial surveys of mountain goats in Mount Rainier National Park, Washington.

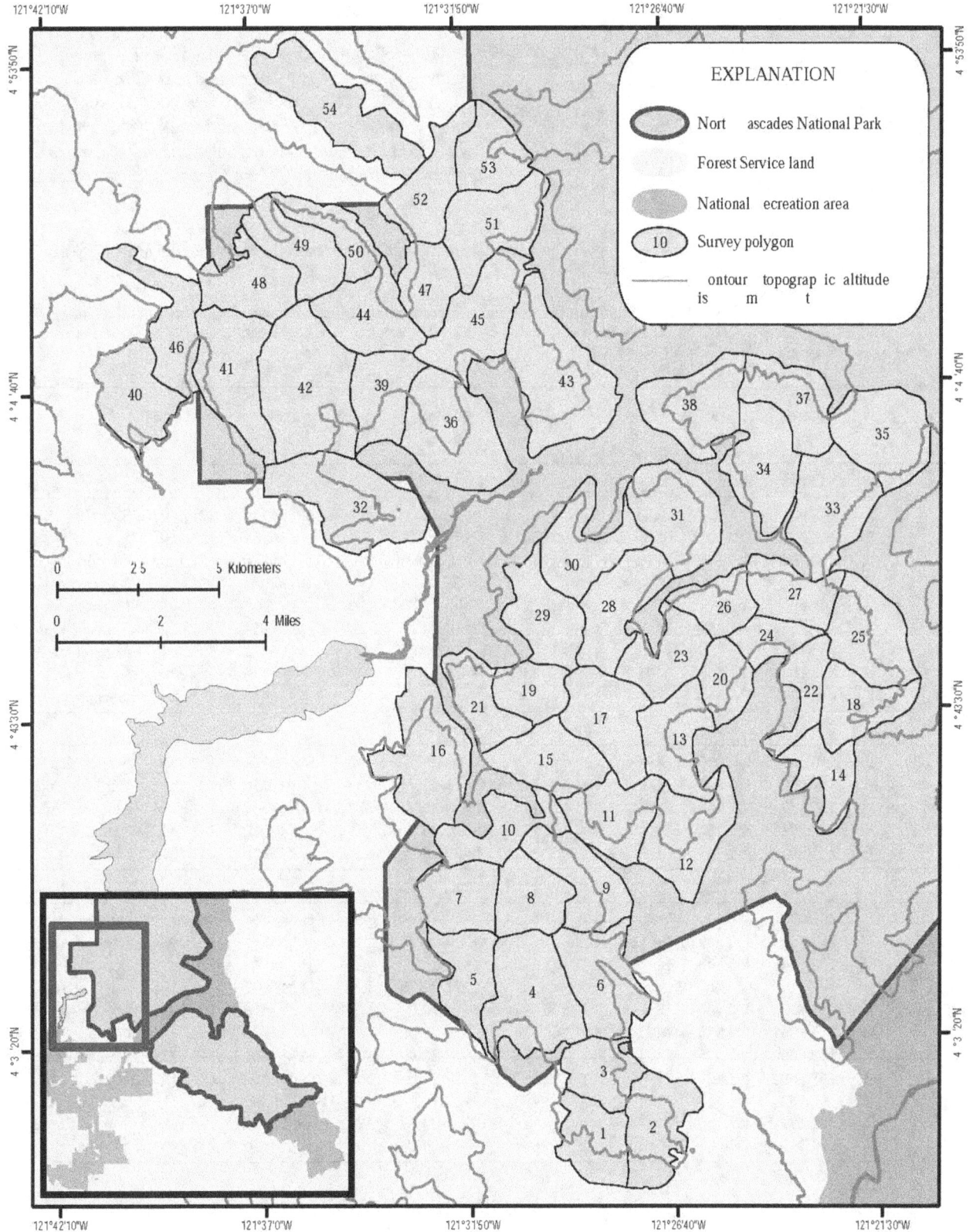

Figure 4. Aerial survey polygons comprising the sampling frame used for aerial surveys of mountain goats in North Cascades National Park, Washington. Note that the polygons encompass predicted mountain goat habitat but survey polygons were flown only as low as the 1,220-m altitude contour.

Results

We captured and collared 9, 5, and 11 mountain goats within or adjacent to Mount Rainier, North Cascades, and Olympic National Parks, respectively (table 1). Specific information on capture and physical characteristics of 20 mountain goats that were captured by NPS and USGS crews and contractors is contained in appendix 1.

Seasonal Distribution

GPS-collared mountain goats provided movement data from the time each was captured until the collar malfunctioned (10), the mountain goat died of natural causes (5), the collar fell off (2) or the study ended (8) (table 2). Two GPS collars failed immediately following capture and produced negligible data. Of the remaining 23, we obtained

Table 1. Mountain goats captured and GPS-collared within or adjacent to Mount Rainier, North Cascades, and Olympic National Parks, Washington, 2003–07.

[Color Code: Bk, Black; Bl, Blue; R, Red; W, White; G, Grey. Three-color combinations represent alternating colors on collar; all battery packs are black. Two-color combinations represent the color of collar and battery pack, respectively. AVID ID, American Veterinary Identification Device. Capture method: GD, ground darting; AD, aerial darting; LN, leg noosing]

Collar identification No.	Sex	VHF freq	UHF freq	Color code	AVID ID	Capture date	Capture method	Capture latitude	Capture longitude	General location
					Mount Rainier National Park					
00550	F	149.049	451.870	Bk-Bl-Y	none	09-18-2003	GD	46.91534	-121.6708	Sunrise
00876	F	162.081	450.700	R-W	081 883 367	09-18-2005	AD	46.86508	-121.5691	Buck Lake
00881	F	162.005	450.100	Bk-W	107 773 365	09-18-2005	AD	46.50780	-121.3650	Goat Rocks
00911	F	149.500	451.020	Y-Bk-Y	none	09-03-2004	GD	46.92563	-121.6686	Mt. Fremont
00917-2	M	149.850	451.090	Bl-Y-Y	none	07-02-2007	GD	46.92975	-121.6635	Mt. Fremont
00936	M	151.753	451.080	R-Bl-Bl	none	08-10-2004	AD	46.94850	-121.4296	Crystal Mountain
01894	M	162.131	450.950	Bl-G	107 352 294	09-18-2005	AD	46.95223	-121.7614	Mineral Mtn.
01900	F	162.194	451.200	Bl-R	107 368 842	09-18-2005	AD	47.00770	-121.3202	Cowlitz Park
01903	F	162.232	451.350	Y-Bl	107 781 020	09-18-2005	AD	46.48950	-121.4036	Ohanapakosh Park
					North Cascades National Park					
00541	F	148.248	451.720	Bk-Y-Y	none	08-09-2003	AD	48.80364	-121.5354	Nooksack
00889	M	162.095	450.800	Bl-Y	107 802 616	09-21-2005	AD	48.42150	-121.3090	Burdeen Lake
01895	F	162.145	451.000	R-G	107 612 776	09-20-2005	AD	48.52230	-121.3186	Shuksan
01897	F	162.155	451.050	Y	107 594 535	09-20-2005	AD	48.47000	-121.7600	Shuksan
01901	F	162.205	451.250	Bl-R	082 580 362	09-20-2005	AD	48.38370	-121.2916	Shuksan
					Olympic National Park					
00877	F	162.072	450.600	Y-R	107 783 851	09-19-2005	AD	unknown	unknown	Mt. Carrie
00882	F	162.014	450.300	R-G	none	08-20-2005	LN	47.58948	-123.2931	Lake of the Angels
00883	M	162.044	450.400	Bl-W	107 563 338	09-19-2005	AD	47.48770	-123.4531	Mt. Olympus
00884	F	162.019	450.200	Y	none	07-21-2005	LN	47.95982	-123.4771	Mt. Angeles
00885	F	162.057	450.500	Bl -G	107 570 092	09-19-2005	AD	47.83500	-123.5875	Mt. Ferry
01891	M	162.106	450.850	Bl-G	107 803 313	09-20-2005	AD	47.41070	-123.2444	Chimney Peak
01892	F	162.120	450.900	Bl-G	107 785 862	09-19-2005	AD	47.88861	-123.6237	Mt. Carrie
01898	M	162.169	451.100	Bl-Y	107 803 584	09-20-2005	AD	47.46180	-123.4120	Mt. Olympus
01899	F	162.182	451.150	Y-G	107 865 798	09-19-2005	AD	47.50800	-123.3116	Ludden Peak
01899-2	M	162.182	451.150	Bk	none	07-03-2007	LN	47.98405	-123.4780	Sunrise Ridge
01902	F	162.217	451.300	R-Bl	107 865 631	09-20-2005	AD	47.46170	-123.4082	Mt. Olympus

location data for a range of 39–751 days (median=616 days; interquartile range=250–722 days; table 2). We obtained a total of 43,473 locations of GPS-collared mountain goats, including 26 percent 2D locations derived from 3 satellites and 74 percent 3D locations derived from ≥4 satellites (table 2).

Fix acquisition rate of GPS collars on mountain goats averaged 61 percent but was highly variable among individual animals and seasons (fig. 5). Variability in fix acquisition rates is taken into consideration in the interpretation of results.

Altitudinal Movements

GPS-collared goats exhibited predictable seasonal patterns of altitudinal movements between winter and summer ranges. Mountain goats used relatively low altitudes from late autumn through spring, and high altitude subalpine and alpine habitats during summer and early autumn (fig. 6). Generally, mountain goats in Mount Rainier National Park

Table 2.   Location data collected from 25 GPS-collared mountain goats in Mount Rainier, North Cascades, and Olympic National Parks, Washington, 2003–08.

Collar identification No.	Sex	Data starting date	Data ending date	Range (days)	Number of locations		Reason for ending data collection
					2D	3D	
Mount Rainier National Park							
00550	F	09-18-2003	05-25-2004	250	172	1,182	Collar failure
00876	F	09-18-2005	09-11-2007	723	587	2,813	End of study
00881	F	09-18-2005	04-22-2006	217	170	394	Mortality
00911	F	09-03-2004	08-10-2005	342	575	1,287	Collar failure
00917-2	M	07-02-2007	08-10-2007	39	20	196	Dropped collar
00936	M	08-17-2004	06-26-2006	687	766	3,262	Collar failure
01894	M	09-18-2005	09-11-2007	723	578	619	End of study
01900	F	09-18-2005	11-16-2005	59	70	202	Collar failure
01903	F	09-18-2005	02-16-2007	515	580	689	Mortality
North Cascades National Park							
00541	F	08-09-2003	08-24-2005	745	544	4,292	Collar failure
00889	M	09-21-2005	01-30-2007	496	561	751	Collar failure
01895	F	09-20-2005	09-12-2007	722	422	309	End of study
01897	F	09-20-2005	09-20-2005	0	0	0	Collar failure
01901	F	09-20-2005	09-12-2007	722	507	918	End of study
Olympic National Park							
00877	F	09-19-2005	09-19-2005	0	0	0	Collar failure
00882	F	08-20-2005	09-11-2007	751	996	2,510	End of study
00883	M	09-19-2005	09-06-2007	717	690	1,527	End of study
00884	F	07-21-2005	06-30-2007	709	852	1,815	Collar failure
00885	F	09-19-2005	05-27-2007	616	838	1,233	Mortality
01891	M	09-20-2005	12-09-2005	80	86	211	Collar failure
01892	F	09-19-2005	09-07-2007	718	701	2,950	End of study
01898	M	09-20-2005	09-11-2007	721	776	1,683	End of study
01899	F	09-19-2005	08-30-2006	345	392	954	Mortality
01899-2	M	07-03-2007	08-27-2008	420	148	2,219	Dropped collar
01902	F	09-20-2005	03-09-2006	170	149	277	Mortality
Totals					11,180	32,293	

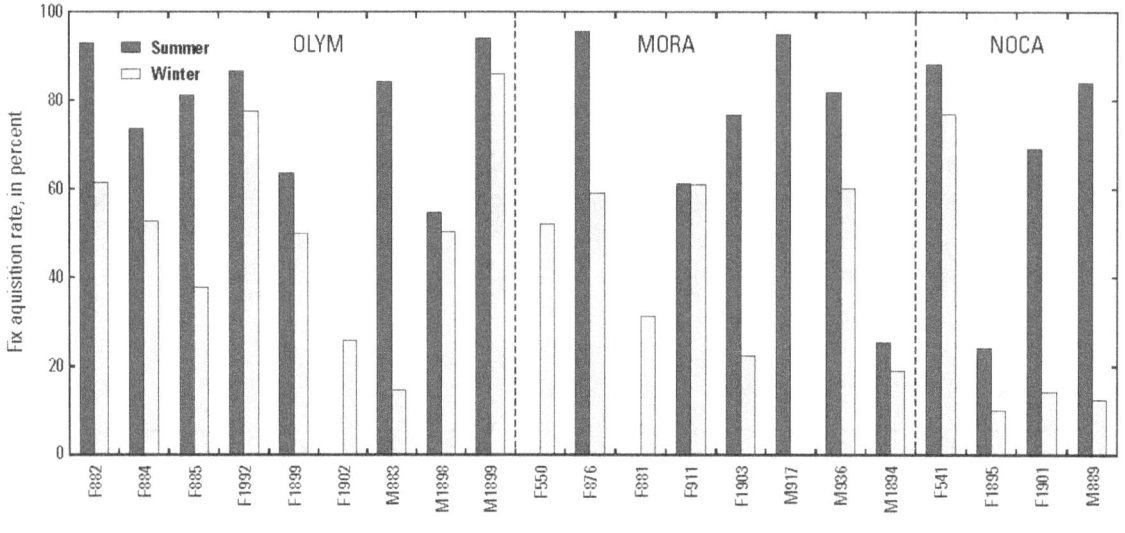

Figure 5. Individual and seasonal variation in the fix acquisition rates of GPS collars on mountain goats in Olympic (OLYM), Mount Rainier (MORA), and North Cascades (NOCA) National Parks, Washington, 2003–08. Mountain goat identifications indicate females (F) and males (M) and the identification number on the GPS collar. Winter is defined as December 15–February 15 and summer is defined as July 15–September 15.

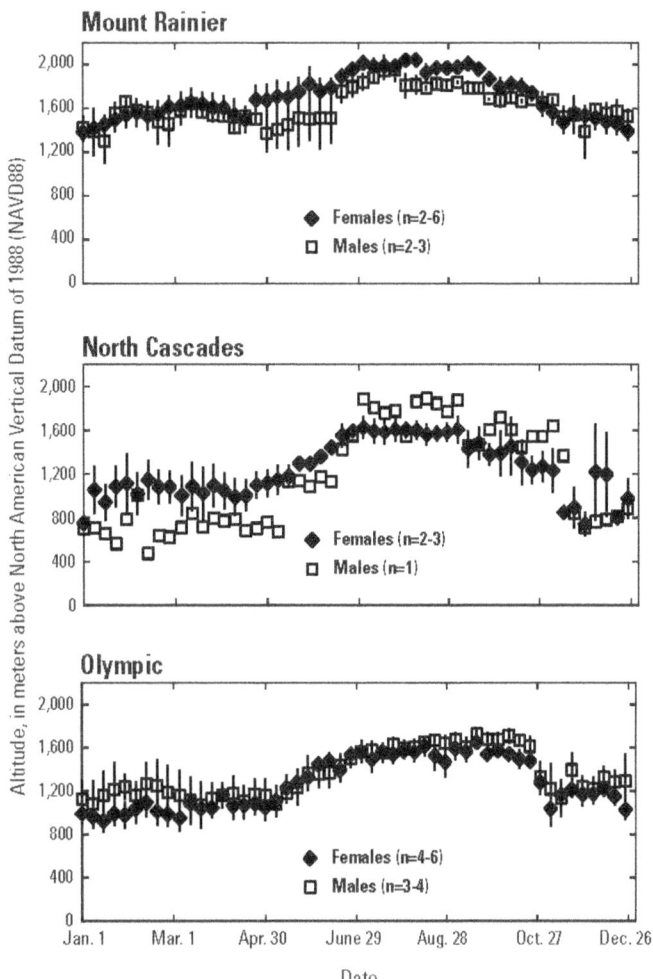

during summer and winter used higher altitudes than mountain goats in North Cascades and Olympic National Parks. There were no clear differences in altitudinal distributions between male and female mountain goats, but differences could be obscured by low sample sizes, particularly for males (fig. 6).

Timing of seasonal transitions between summer and winter ranges varied among individuals (fig. 7). Due to sample size constraints, we were unable to discriminate differences among parks in the seasonal timing of altitudinal movements of mountain goats. Data pooled among parks indicated that the median date of seasonal transition to summer range was June 11 for females and June 19 for males, although these transition dates ranged from April 24 to July 3 for both males and females. The median date of transition from summer to winter range was October 26 for females and November 9 for males, but these dates ranged from September 11 to December 16 for females and from September 28 to December 23 for males. Although females typically moved to summer and winter ranges over a week earlier than males, both sexes were on winter ranges approximately equal durations, generally more than 200 days (fig. 7).

Figure 6. Weekly mean altitudes (+SE) of male and female GPS-collared mountain goats in Mount Rainier, North Cascades, and Olympic National Parks, Washington, 2003–08.

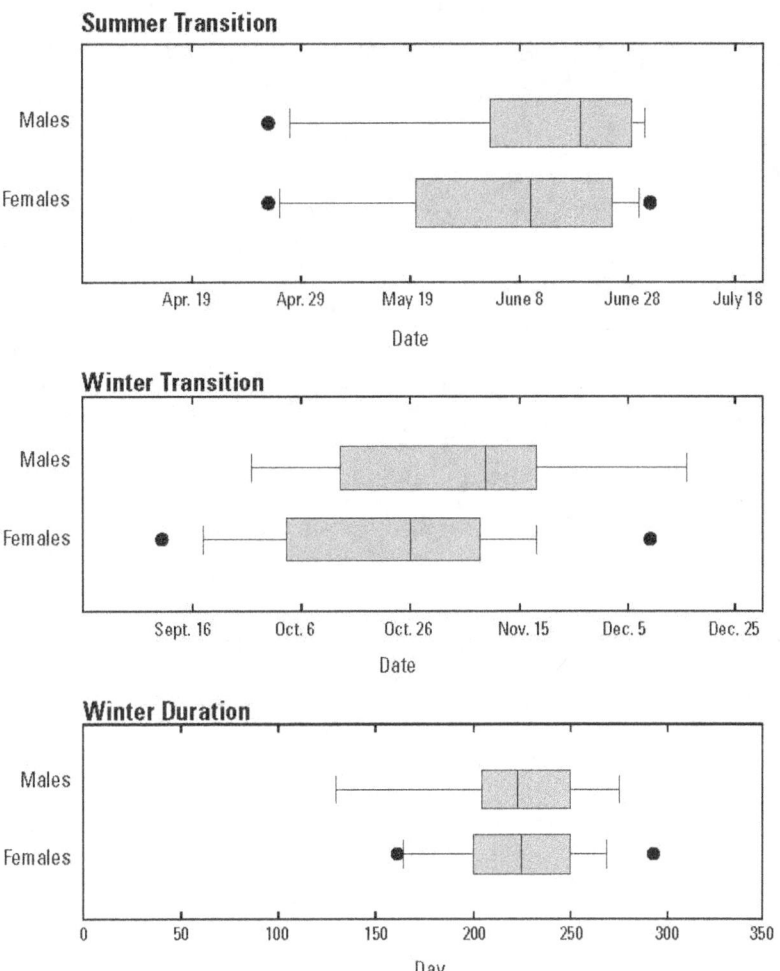

Figure 7. Distributions of dates that GPS-collared mountain goats made transitions between summer and winter ranges and the duration of winter range use (days) by male and female mountain goats in Mount Rainier, North Cascades, and Olympic National Parks, Washington, 2003–08. Each box shows the 25th–75th percentiles with the median in the middle. Whiskers extend from the 10th to 90th percentile and outlying records are shown as dots.

Altitudinal distributions also varied among individuals within seasons (fig. 8). Median altitudes used by individual GPS-collared goats ranged from 817 to 1,541 m during winter in Olympic and North Cascades National Parks, and from 1,215 to 1,787 m during winter in Mount Rainier. By contrast, median altitudes used by GPS-collared goats during summer ranged from 1,312 to 1,819 m in Olympic and North Cascades National Parks and 1,780 to 2,061 m in Mount Rainier National Park (fig. 8).

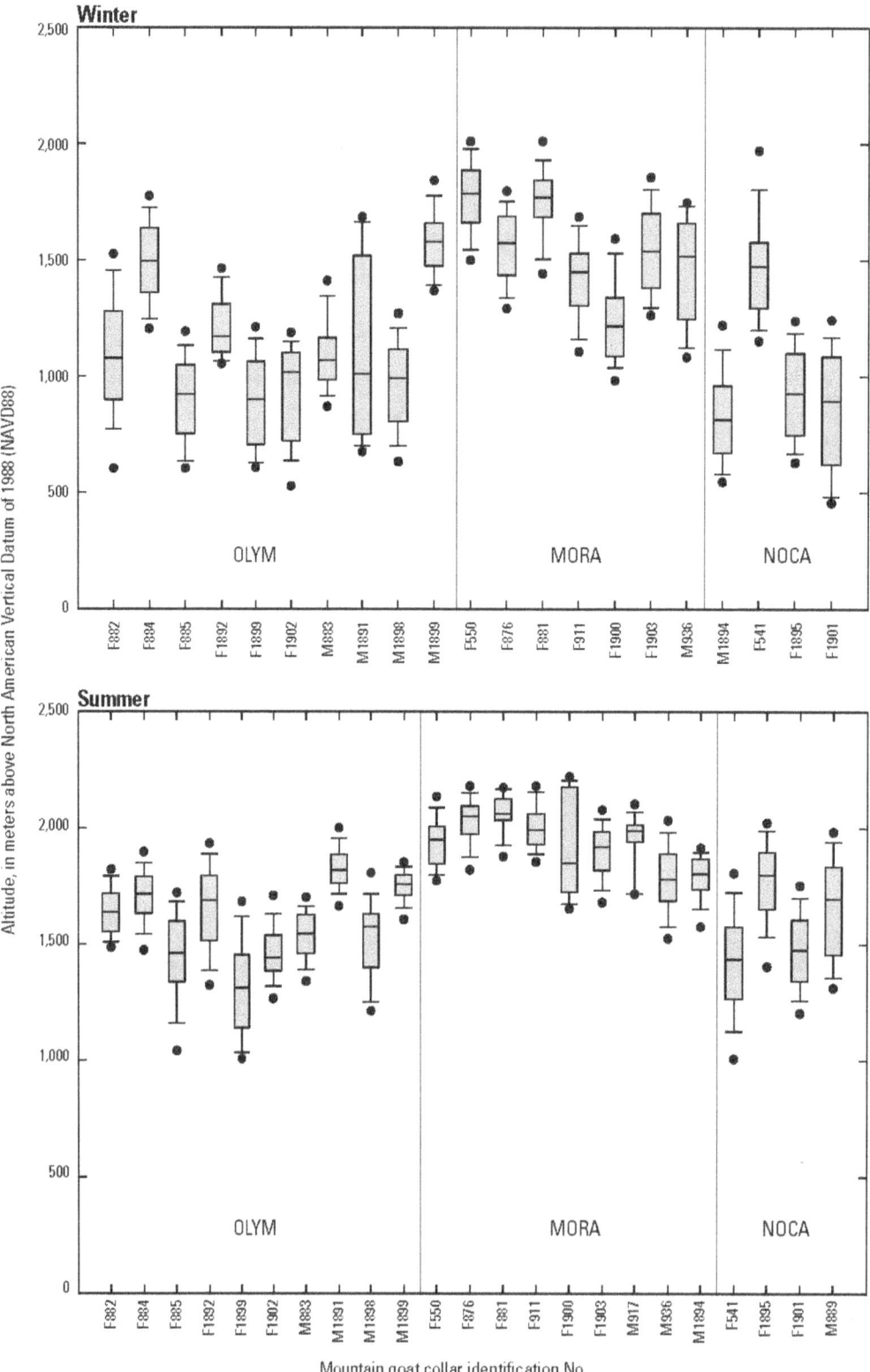

Figure 8. Distribution of altitude records for individual GPS-collared mountain goats in Olympic (OLYM), Mount Rainier (MORA), and North Cascades (NOCA) National Parks, Washington, during summers and winters, 2003–08. Mountain goat collar identifications indicate females (F) and males (M) and the identification number on the GPS collar. Each box shows the 25th and 75th percentile of altitudes with the median in the middle. Whiskers extend from the 10th to 90th percentile and outlying records are shown as dots.

Use of Mountain Goat Survey Areas During Summer

Altitudinal distributions of GPS-collared mountain goats did not differ appreciably across the 24-hour cycle during July 10–31, the primary survey season (fig. 9). Overlapping standard errors of the estimated hourly mean altitudes used by GPS-collared goats indicated that diurnal variations in altitudinal distribution were not statistically significant ($P > 0.05$). The proportions of GPS-collared mountain goats within the survey sampling frame varied among parks (fig. 10), reflecting differences in altitudinal distributions of GPS-collared mountain goats among parks (fig. 6) as well as differences in the methods used to define the sampling

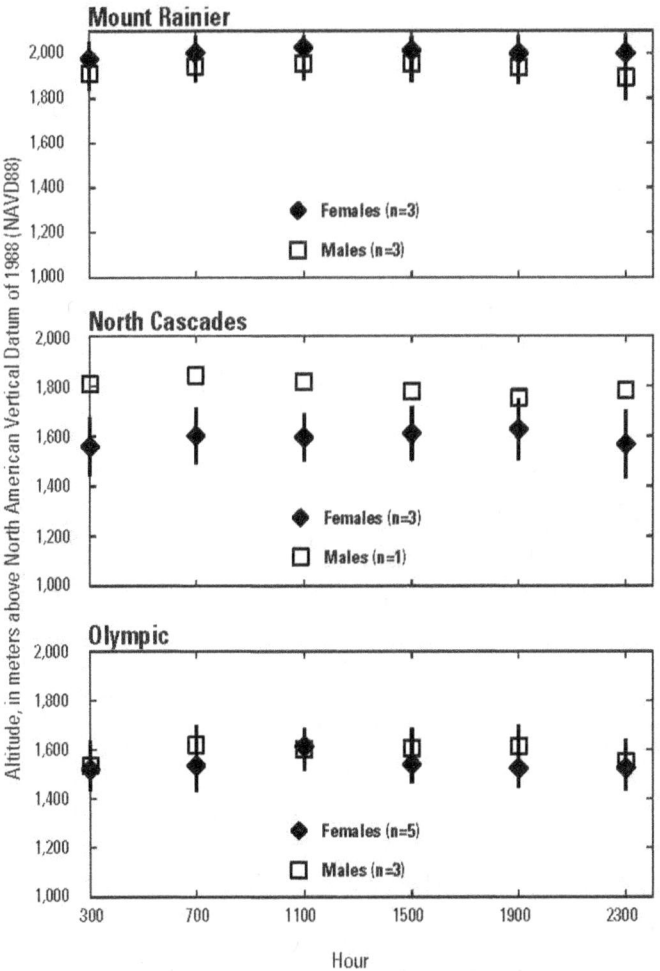

Figure 9. Selected hourly mean altitudes (+SE) of male and female GPS-collared mountain goats in Mount Rainier, North Cascades, and Olympic National Parks, Washington, July 10–31, 2003–08.

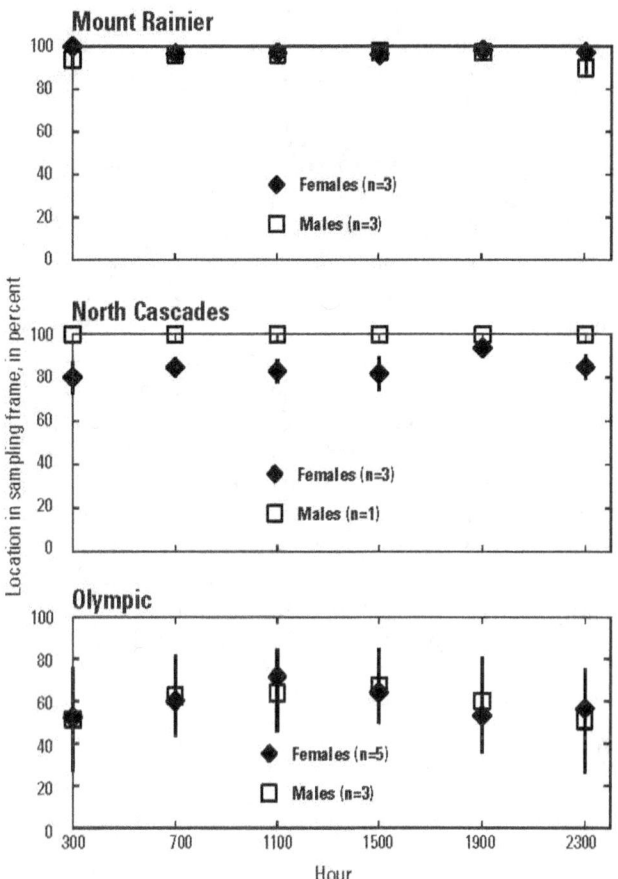

Figure 10. Selected hourly mean percentage (+SE) of GPS-telemetry locations of collared mountain goats within the mountain goat survey sampling frames in Mount Rainier, North Cascades, and Olympic National Parks, Washington, July 10–31, 2003–08.

frames. Mountain goats in Mount Rainier National Park typically were present at altitudes greater than 1,800 m and were within the sampling frame nearly 100 percent of the time. Mountain goats in North Cascades National Park typically were present at altitudes greater than 1,500 m and were within the sampling frame more than 80 percent of the time (fig. 10). Mountain goats in Olympic National Park generally were present at altitudes greater than 1,400 m and were within the sampling frame less frequently than in Mount Rainier and North Cascades National Parks (fig. 10).

High variation in the percentage of mountain goat locations within the survey frame in Olympic National Park warranted a closer evaluation of their altitudinal distribution. Because staff at Olympic National Park typically conduct surveys of mountain goats in the morning hours from 6:00 to 10:00, we focused attention on locations of mountain goats obtained at 7:00 and 11:00, the hours that most collars were scheduled to obtain GPS locations. Altitudinal locations of GPS-collared mountain goats during those morning hours within the primary survey season (July 10–31) ranged from 1,025 to 2,010 m. The sampling frame, defined at the lower limit by the 1,520-m altitude contour, contained approximately 70 percent of the locations of GPS-collared mountain goats in Olympic National Park, and thus excluded approximately 30 percent (fig. 11). Because the sampling frame boundary cut through the 30th percentile of the altitudinal distribution of mountain goats in Olympic National Park, relatively small variations in altitudinal distributions of mountain goats were magnified to larger variations in proportions of animals present within the survey sampling frames (figs. 9 and 10).

We fit a global model and several plausible candidate models to estimate the probability that GPS collared mountain goats were present within the aerial survey sampling frame in Olympic National Park (table 3).

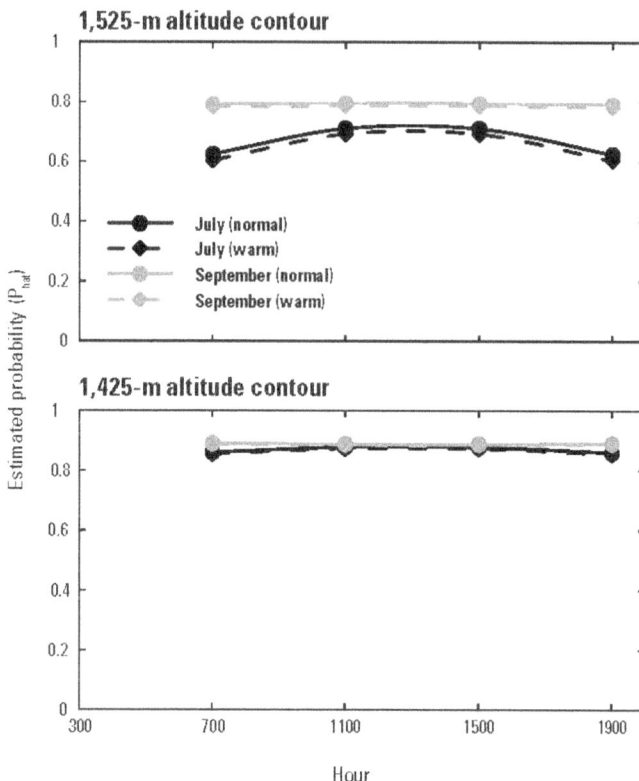

Figure 12. Estimated probability (P_{hat}) that GPS-collared mountain goats were within aerial survey sampling areas defined at the lower altitude by 1,525-m and 1,425-m altitude contours in Olympic National Park, Washington, July and September, 2005–08. P_{hat} is estimated based on logistic regression models with parameters defined in tables 4 and 6. Note that lines denoting normal and warm temperatures are nearly indistinguishable (superimposed) for survey areas delineated at the lower altitude by the 1,425-m altitude contour.

Global and candidate models included combinations of the variables diurnal period (crepuscular versus midday), daily mean temperature (°C), and survey season (July versus September). The global model and most of the candidate models explained significant variation in the presence of GPS-collared mountain goats within the sampling frame (table 3). The estimated variance inflation factor was near 1 ($\hat{c}$=1.42) indicating acceptable model structure and a lack of overdispersion (Burnham and Anderson, 2002). Hence, we opted not to apply an overdispersion adjustment to expand variance estimates.

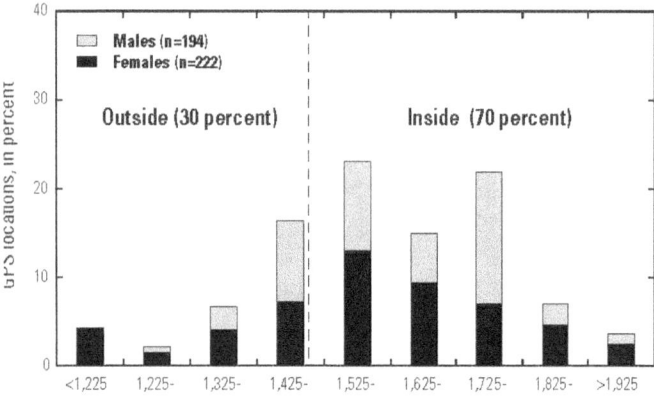

Figure 11. Altitudinal distribution of GPS-collared mountain goats during morning hours (0700–1100) in Olympic National Park, July 10–31, 2005–08. Dashed line represents altitude boundary delineating locations of mountain goats that were inside versus outside of the sampling frame.

Table 3. Candidate logistic regression models and associated statistics for predicting probabilities that GPS-collared mountain goats were present within the aerial survey sampling area in Olympic National Park, Washington, July and September, 2005–08.

[The sampling area was delineated at the lower altitude by the 1,525-meter altitude contour. Candidate models: Diurnal period (DP) is a dichotomous variable for dawn/dusk (0) or midday (1); dawn/dusk is defined as 0500–0900 and 1701–2100 hours; midday is defined as 0901–1700 hours; season (SEAS) is a dichotomous variable for July (0) or September (1); temperature (TEMP) is 24-hour average temperature (°C) measured at 1,525-meter altitude. K, number of parameters that can be estimated; AIC, Akaike's information criterion; w_i, Akaike's weight; Δ, change]

Candidate models	K	AIC	ΔAIC	w_i	Likelihood ratio (X^2)	P
DP, SEAS, DP*SEAS	4	1801.40	0.00	0.37	46.60	<0.0001
DP, SEAS	3	1801.85	0.45	0.29	44.20	<0.0001
DP, SEAS, TEMP, DP*SEAS	5	1802.92	1.53	0.17	47.13	<0.0001
DP, SEAS, TEMP	4	1803.36	1.96	0.14	47.70	<0.0001
SEAS	2	1806.22	4.83	0.03	37.82	<0.0001
DP, TEMP	3	1824.20	22.81	<0.01	21.80	<0.0001
TEMP	2	1828.24	26.85	<0.01	15.80	<0.0001
DP	2	1837.90	36.51	<0.01	6.09	0.01

We identified four plausible models for predicting mountain goat presence within the survey sampling area, based on the convention that models with ΔAIC less than 4 are considered plausible (Burnham and Anderson, 2002). We averaged parameters for each of the covariates based on model weights of the four top-ranked and plausible models (table 4; Burnham and Anderson, 2002). Model predictions for mountain goat presence within the sampling frame ranged from 0.62 during crepuscular periods in July to 0.79 in September (fig. 12). Predicted mountain goat presence within the sampling frame was greater during September than July,

and diurnal variation in mountain goat presence was greater during July than September. During July, mountain goats were more likely to be present within the sampling frame during midday than during early morning or late evening. High temperatures had only a minor negative influence on the predicted mountain goat presence within the survey area during July (fig. 12).

Because mountain goat presence within the defined sampling area was sensitive to relatively small altitudinal movements, we created a hypothetical sampling area by reducing the lower altitude boundary 100 m to the 1,425-m altitude contour to explore the potential influence of minor adjustments to the survey area boundaries on the likelihood of mountain goat presence. We examined the same set of candidate models as previously to determine the influence of diurnal period, season, and air temperature on the likelihood of mountain goat presence within the hypothetical survey area (table 5). In contrast to the previous analysis, none of the candidate models nor any of the model-averaged covariate parameter estimates was significant (P>0.05; tables 5 and 6), indicating that mountain goat presence within the revised sampling frame was influenced negligibly by diurnal period, season, or air temperature. Predicted probabilities of mountain goat presence within the revised sampling area, based on model-averaged parameters from all eight models (table 6), ranged from 0.86 to 0.90 percent (fig. 12).

Table 4. Model-averaged logistic regression parameters (B_i) for estimating probabilities that GPS-collared mountain goats were present within the aerial survey sampling area in Olympic National Park, Washington, July and September, 2005–08.

[The sampling area was delineated at the lower altitude by the 1,525-meter altitude contour. B_i, model-averaged logistic regression parameter i, SE, standard error; z, normal deviate; P, probability of z]

Parameter	B_i	SE	z	P
Intercept	0.607	0.143	4.24	<0.001
Diurnal period (DP)	0.386	0.164	2.35	0.019
Season (SEAS)	0.785	0.168	4.67	<0.001
Temperature	-0.010	0.084	-0.119	0.904
DP*SEAS	-0.366	0.234	-1.56	0.156

Table 5.   Candidate logistic regression models and associated statistics for predicting probabilities that GPS-collared mountain goats were present within a hypothetical survey area in Olympic National Park, Washington, July and September, 2005–08.

[The hypothetical area was delineated at the lower altitude by the 1,425-meter altitude contour. Candidate models: Diurnal period (DP) is a dichotomous variable for dawn/dusk (0) or midday (1); dawn/dusk is defined as 0500–0900 and 1701–2100 hours; midday is defined as 0901–1700 hours; season (SEAS) is a dichotomous variable for July (0) or September (1); temperature (TEMP) is 24-hour average temperature (°C) measured at 1,525 meter altitude. K, number of parameters that can be estimated; AIC, Akaike's information criterion; w_i, Akaike's weight; Δ, change]

Candidate models	K	AIC	ΔAIC	w_i	Likelihood ratio (X^2)	P
SEAS	2	1205.70	0.00	0.33	2.56	0.11
DP, SEAS	3	1206.92	1.22	0.18	3.39	0.18
DP	2	1207.50	1.80	0.14	0.82	0.36
TEMP	2	1207.90	2.20	0.11	0.45	0.50
DP, SEAS, DP*SEAS	4	1208.57	2.87	0.08	3.73	0.29
DP, SEAS, TEMP	4	1208.85	3.15	0.07	3.46	0.33
DP, TEMP	3	1209.05	3.35	0.06	1.26	0.53
DP, SEAS, TEMP, DP*SEAS	5	1210.50	4.80	0.03	3.81	0.43

Table 6.   Model-averaged logistic regression parameters (B_i) for estimating probabilities that GPS-collared mountain goats were present within a hypothetical survey area in Olympic National Park, Washington, July and September, 2005–08.

[The hypothetical sampling area was delineated at the lower altitude by the 1,425-meter altitude contour. B_i, model-averaged logistic regression parameter i; SE, standard error; z, normal deviate; P, probability of z]

Parameter	B_i	SE	z	P
Intercept	1.873	0.164	11.42	<0.001
Diurnal Period (DP)	0.156	0.169	0.92	0.36
Survey Season (SEAS)	0.260	0.167	1.56	0.12
Temperature	-0.005	0.018	-0.28	0.78
DP*SEAS	-0.180	0.306	-0.59	0.56

Seasonal Home Range Utilization Distributions

Seasonal home ranges of male and female GPS-collared mountain goats were highly variable (fig. 13). Adaptive kernel home ranges (95 percent UD) of eight GPS-collared males ranged from 1.6 to 37.0 km² during summers and 3.6–7.5 km² during winters, although that distribution is skewed during summer due to one dispersing male whose summer range expanded considerably during the study (fig. 13, see also M936, appendixes 2–3). Home range distributions of 15 females ranged from 2.8 to 16.4 km² during summer and 0.7 to 9.5 km² during winter. The interquartile range during summer, which defines the central tendency of 50 percent of the sample, ranged from about 2.7 to 11.6 km² for males, and 6.2 to 8.6 km² for females. During winter, this central tendency in home range size ranged from 4.4 to 6.8 km² for males and 1.4 to 3.8 km² for females.

Aerial Surveys

We completed sightability trial surveys on 18 days between July 10 and September 6, 2006 and 2007, primarily between July 10 and July 31 each year (table 7). We surveyed nearly 184, 136, and 191 km2 of mountain goat habitat during sightability trials in Mount Rainier, North Cascades, and Olympic National Parks, respectively (table 7). Survey intensity averaged 3.7–3.8 minutes/km² in Mount Rainier and North Cascades National Parks, and 6.2 minutes/km² in Olympic National Park. Maps of surveyed and partially surveyed polygons are shown in appendix 4.

We detected 318 groups of mountain goats and 878 individuals during sightability surveys (table 8). Average group sizes of mountain goats were larger in Mountain Rainier National Park (mean=5.6, range=1–39) than in North Cascades and Olympic National Parks (means=2.1–2.2, range=1–14), as determined from non-overlapping 95-percent confidence intervals (P<0.05; table 8). Because it is difficult to reliably distinguish male from female mountain goats from the air, we did not discern population compositions. The percentage of young of the year (that is, kids) among sighted mountain goats, however, averaged approximately 18–20 percent of the population, and did not differ among parks (X^2=0.59, 2 df, P=0.74; table 8).

Mean detection probabilities of mountain goat groups, computed from the aerial sightability model (Rice and others, 2009), ranged from 0.64 to 0.73 in the three national parks and were lowest in North Cascades National Park (table 9). Mean detection probabilities estimated for individuals were higher than for groups because individual means were estimated as the mean detection probability of groups weighted by the number of individuals present within each group and a disproportionate number of individuals were present in the more easily sighted larger groups (Rice and others, 2009). The mean sightabilities of individual goats ranged from 0.69 to 0.87 in the three parks and were highest in Mount Rainier National Park and lowest in North Cascades National Park.

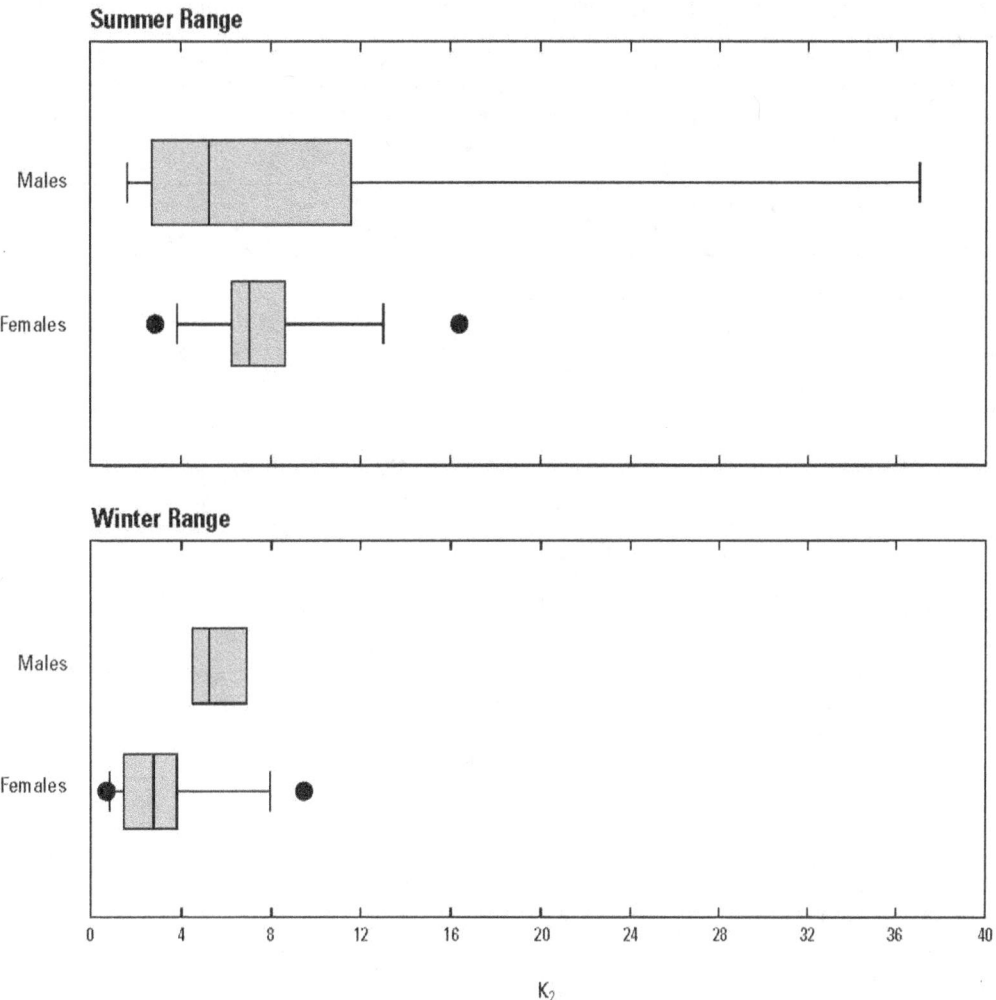

Figure 13. Distributions of summer and winter home range sizes (95-percent adaptive kernel utilization distributions) of male and female GPS-collared mountain goats in Mount Rainier, North Cascades, and Olympic National Parks, Washington, 2003–08. Each box shows the 25th–75th percentiles with the median home range size in the middle. Whiskers extend from the 10th to 90th percentile and outlying records are shown as dots (except for males during winter, when there were not sufficient home ranges to compute 10th and 90th percentile whiskers. Home range sizes of individual GPS-collared mountain goats are shown in appendix 2).

Table 7.   Summary of aerial surveys conducted as sightability trials in Mount Rainier, North Cascades, and Olympic National Parks, Washington, summer 2006–07.

[Results for individual polygons are provided in <u>appendix 5</u>. Survey duration: Time spent surveying designated polygons, excluding time spent commuting between polygons and time required after completing a survey to locate missed goats and obtain covariates for missed goats. Survey intensity: Survey duration divided by survey area. km², square kilometers; min, minutes]

Survey date	Polygons surveyed	Area (km²)	Survey duration (min)	Survey intensity (min/km²)
Mount Rainier National Park				
07-17-2006	[1]12, [1]13, 18, 29, 30	24.5	98.7	4.0
07-31-2006	1–9, 11, 13, 18, 23, 26	68.0	245.0	3.6
08-01-2006	17, 29, 30	16.6	49.4	3.0
07-11-2007	16–18, [1]26, 28, 29	37.2	144.5	3.9
07-24-2007	17, 23, 26	16.7	66.9	4.0
07-25-2007	28, 29, 30	20.9	85.9	4.1
Subtotals		183.8	690.4	3.8
North Cascades National Park				
07-18-2006	[1]3, 4, [1]5, 6, 9, 33, 34, 52, [1]54	46.7	197.8	4.2
08-02-2006	6, [1]28, [1]54	20.4	36.8	1.8
07-12-2007	6, [1]9, 42, 54	30.6	98.1	3.2
07-26-2007	4, 6, 8, 9, [1]52, 54	37.9	168.8	4.5
Subtotals		135.6	501.6	3.7
Olympic National Park				
07-10-2006	126, 128, 131, 132, 134, 135, 139, [1]5, [1]9, [1]10, 141, 142	31.6	197.4	6.2
07-11-2006	69, 78, 93, 123	20.7	203.7	9.8
07-24-2006	4–11, 123, 125, 126, 128, 137, 139, 142	39.5	130.7	3.3
07-26-2006	93, 94, 131, 132, 135, 136	20.3	121.4	6.0
07-09-2007	[1]5, [1]9, [1]10, 90, 93, 127N, [1]128	17.8	134.1	7.5
07-10-2007	69, 78, [1]123	15.5	79.6	5.1
07-16-2007	4–11, 93, 123, 126, 127N, 128	35.2	250.5	7.1
09-06-2007	[1]5–7, [1]9–11, [1]122E, [1]123W	10.3	65.0	6.3
Subtotals		190.9	1,182.4	6.2

[1]Incomplete polygon(s) surveyed. Areas are adjusted for computation of survey intensity.

Table 8. Group size, counts, and composition of mountain goats observed from aerial surveys conducted as sightability trials in Mount Rainier, North Cascades, and Olympic National Parks, Washington, summer 2006–07.

[Results for individual polygons are provided as appendix 5. Counts: Proportions of kids and adults (for example, total-kids) do not differ among parks (X^2=0.59, 2 d.f., P=0.74). Composition: SE, standard error of binomial distribution (Zar, 1984, p. 377). N, number; SE, standard error; Unk, unknown; %, percent]

Date	Polygons surveyed	Group size				Counts			Composition	
		N	Mean	SE	Range	Total	Kids	Unk	Kids (%)	SE
	Mount Rainier National Park									
07-17-2006	[1]12, [1]13, 18, 29, 30	11	5.5	1.4	1–15	61	15	0	25	5.6
07-31-2006	1–9, 11, 13, 18, 23, 26	16	4.5	1.6	1–22	72	14	0	19	4.7
08-01-2006	17, 29, 30	4	12.3	9.0	1–39	49	10	0	20	5.8
07-11-2007	16–18, [1]26, 28, 29	11	4.4	2.0	1–23	48	6	0	13	4.8
07-24-2007	17, 23, 26	10	9.2	3.6	1–39	92	17	0	18	4.1
07-25-2007	28, 29, 30	7	1.4	0.3	1–3	10	0	0	0	0.0
	Subtotals	59	5.6	1.1	1–39	332	62	0	19	2.1
	North Cascades National Park									
07-18-2006	[1]3, 4, [1]5, 6, 9, 33, 34, 52, [1]54	17	1.8	0.3	1–5	30	5	3	17	6.9
08-02-2006	6, [1]28, [1]54	9	2.4	0.6	1–6	22	4	0	18	8.4
07-12-2007	6, [1]9, 42, 54	22	2.7	0.5	1–10	59	13	0	22	5.4
07-26-2007	4, 6, 8, 9, [1]52, 54	17	2.0	0.4	1–8	34	4	0	12	5.6
	Subtotals	65	2.2	0.2	1–10	145	26	3	18	3.2
	Olympic National Park									
07-10-2006	126, 128, 131, 132, 134, 135, 139, [1]5, [1]9, [1]10, 141, 142	29	2.0	0.4	1–11	57	10	0	18	5.1
07-11-2006	69, 78, 93, 123	46	1.8	0.2	1–5	84	14	0	17	4.1
07-24-2006	4–11, 123, 125, 126, 128, 137, 139, 142	24	1.9	0.3	1–7	46	9	1	20	5.9
07-26-2006	93, 94, 131, 132, 135, 136	13	2.3	0.7	1–10	30	5	0	17	6.9
07-09-2007	[1]5, [1]9, [1]10, 90, 93, 127N, [1]128	19	2.5	0.7	1–14	47	12	0	26	6.4
07-10-2007	69, 78, [1]123	23	1.8	0.2	1–5	42	9	0	21	6.4
07-16-2007	4–11, 93, 123, 126, 127N, 128	32	2.7	0.5	1–10	86	23	0	27	4.8
09-06-2007	[1]5–7, [1]9–11, [1]122E, [1]123W	8	1.1	0.1	1–2	9	0	0	0	0.0
	Subtotals	194	2.1	0.1	1–14	401	82	1	20	2.0

[1]Incomplete polygon(s) surveyed.

Table 9. Number of groups counted, total mountain goats counted, and mean sightability of groups and individual mountain goats in Mount Rainier, North Cascades, and Olympic National Parks, Washington, summer 2006–07.

[Mean sightability, groups: Mean probability of sighting groups of mountain goats. Mean sightability, individuals: Mean probability of sighting individuals computed as the mean probability of sighting groups weighted by number of individuals within each]

National Park unit	Groups	Total	Mean sightability	
			Groups	Individuals
Mount Rainier	59	332	0.73	0.87
North Cascades	65	145	0.64	0.69
Olympic	194	401	0.72	0.76

Discussion

Seasonal patterns of altitudinal movement of mountain goats within the three parks were consistent with seasonal patterns reported previously for mountain goats throughout the Cascade Range in Washington (Rice, 2008). Our results corroborate high variability in altitudinal movements among individual goats, as well as within and between seasons (Rice, 2008). We identified seasonal ranges of mountain goats on the basis of their seasonal altitudinal shifts in distribution, although there was considerable overlap in seasonal distributions that appeared to be influenced by short-term variations in snow pack and weather conditions. Mountain goats moved upward in altitude as snow conditions permitted during winter, but generally used lower altitudes during winter than during summer. Our results confirmed that although generally considered an alpine species, mountain goats use habitats at a wide variety of altitudes annually, including montane habitats at comparatively low altitudes during a long winter season (Rice, 2008).

Our results are the first to describe seasonal altitudinal movements of GPS-collared mountain goats in the Olympic Mountains, Washington. The distribution of mountain goats in the Olympic Mountains was comparable to altitude profiles of mountain goats in North Cascades National Park but mountain goats used lower altitudes in the Olympic Mountains than in Mount Rainier National Park (fig. 6), which we interpret as reflecting the lower altitude of preferred subalpine habitats in the Olympic Mountains and North Cascades than in Mount Rainier National Park. There were no obvious differences in the seasonal patterns of altitude use among the three parks and the observed patterns were similar to those seen throughout the Cascade Range (Rice, 2008).

A primary motivation for examining seasonal and diurnal variations in altitudinal distributions was to evaluate the adequacy of sampling designs used to survey mountain goats in each park. Movements of mountain goats beyond the boundaries of the sampling areas may bias population estimates, particularly in Olympic National Park where mountain goats were most frequently outside the survey areas, and to lesser extents in North Cascades and Mount Rainier National Parks. We do not feel that sample sizes of GPS-collared mountain goats available for this study were sufficient to estimate the magnitude of such availability biases precisely (see fig. 10), but the greatest biases appeared evident in Olympic National Park where the census zone excluded lands at altitudes below 1,520 m (Houston and others, 1986). The lower altitude boundary was based on movements of goats previously studied primarily in the Klahhane Ridge area of Olympic National Park (Stevens, 1979; Houston and others, 1986). Although we confirmed that GPS-collared mountain goats in the Klahhane Ridge area primarily used altitudes

above 1,520 m (see F884, M1899-2, fig. 8), other GPS-collared mountain goats used lower altitudes, suggesting that segments of the park-wide population are not reliably present within the sampled areas. The more generous delineations of survey zones in North Cascades National Park (habitats at altitudes above 1,400 m) and Mount Rainier National Park (no altitude constraint on habitats) more reliably sampled those entire populations.

Historically, mountain goat surveys have been conducted in Olympic National Park during early mornings in mid- to late-July because previous studies indicated that was when mountain goats were most reliably found in open habitats above timberline, and because it was suspected that excessive temperatures may drive goats down to forests at lower altitudes outside the survey boundaries (Houston and others, 1986, 1994b). Although mountain goats in Olympic National Park frequently crossed in and out of the survey units diurnally, they were more commonly in the survey units during midday than during the early morning foraging periods, contrary to expectations (fig. 10). That pattern may reflect the tendency for mountain goats to bed down and rest during midday in rocky bluff habitats that typically occur higher in altitude than productive subalpine foraging areas (Stevens, 1979). Mountain goats were more likely to descend below the survey unit boundaries during July than September, when there also might exist a more pronounced altitudinal gradient in early season forage production. We found little empirical evidence of seasonal or diurnal variations in altitudinal distributions of mountain goats that influenced their presence within the aerial survey boundaries of Mount Rainier and North Cascades National Parks (figs. 6, 9, and 10).

Diurnal distribution patterns of mountain goats do not explain the low counts of mountain goats reported previously during hot summer conditions in Olympic National Park (Houston and others, 1994b). This may reflect the relatively moderate ambient air temperatures that generally prevailed during our study, particularly in comparison to record air temperatures recorded in 1994. Alternatively, microhabitat selection for topographic features during hot weather also may have affected sightability (Rice and others, 2009). Following sightability trials, we occasionally radio tracked those mountain goats missed during a survey to very rugged terrain features, including ice or rock caves and crevices, where goats were very difficult to detect from the air.

Fix acquisition rates of GPS collars were highly variable within all the parks, but within the range reported previously for mountain goats in the Cascades Range (Wells, 2006). Fix acquisition rates were lowest in North Cascades National Park, but that could be related to the small sample of GPS collared mountain goats there, and the influence of low GPS reception of F1895 in particular (fig. 5). GPS collars successfully acquired fixes less frequently during winter than during summer, consistent with previous findings that GPS reception is obstructed most frequently at lower altitudes and in habitats with more overstory vegetation (Wells, 2006). The apparent disparity of fix acquisition rates related to altitude and vegetation suggests that we consistently underestimated use of lower altitude forests by mountain goats. Hence, actual use of low altitude habitats by mountain goats may be greater than depicted and mountain goats may spend more time outside the aerial survey areas than estimated.

In our companion paper, we reported that aerial detection probabilities of GPS-collared mountain goats varied as functions of group size, vegetation cover, and terrain obstruction (Rice and others, 2009). Sightability models applied in Mount Rainier, North Cascades, and Olympic National Parks predicted that detection probabilities of individual mountain goats averaged 0.87, 0.69, and 0.76, respectively (table 9). Higher sightability in Mount Rainier National Park likely reflected the larger groups of mountain goats found there (table 8), as well as more open vegetation conditions.

Those estimates represent true detection biases within the sampled populations, but they may underestimate biases at the population level if not all the population is represented in the survey (Pollock and others, 2004; Rice and others, 2009). Our results indicate that both detection and availability biases related to altitudinal movements of mountain goats likely would affect population estimates in Olympic and to a lesser extent North Cascades National Parks. Detection efficiency measured in Olympic National Park (about 76 percent) combined with biases associated with movements of mountain goats outside the survey frame (about 60–80 percent) supports the previous assertion that the preliminary estimate of detection efficiency used in Olympic National Park (66 percent) was likely conservative at the population level (Houston and others, 1986).

Home ranges of GPS-collared mountain goats are minimum estimates of seasonal areas used by mountain goats. Kernel home range estimates are influenced by the choice of bandwidth used in the estimation (Gitzen and others, 2006; Horne and Garton, 2006; Laver and Kelly, 2008). Undersmoothing, resulting from the use of a narrow kernel bandwidth, may have contributed to the discontinuous home ranges observed for several mountain goats and underestimated home range size (see appendix 3 for visual examples). Biases in the ability of GPS collars to determine positions in low-altitude coniferous forests may have increased fragmentation of the observed utilization distributions and further underestimated home range sizes. Hence, our graphical presentations of home ranges of the GPS-collared mountain goats and the resulting home range estimates are most useful for park managers in identifying key areas used by mountain goats, rather than comparing space-use patterns across studies.

Management Implications

Adjusting raw survey counts of mountain goats for detection biases will reduce but not eliminate biases of mountain goat population estimates derived from aerial surveys in Washington's mountainous national parks. Movements of mountain goats outside the survey areas introduced additional biases in population estimates that cannot be accounted for through detection modeling. Even after applying the detection bias models (Rice and others, 2009), the resulting population estimates must be considered conservative (that is, minimum estimates) because only the population segment that occurs within the defined survey frame is estimated. The potential for underestimating populations of mountain goats is greatest in Olympic National Park where goats move across survey area boundaries, and least in Mount Rainier National Park, where nearly all GPS-collared mountain goats were present within the sampling areas.

Biases in population estimates related to animal distribution or availability are most problematic for trend detection when the proportion of the population available to the survey fluctuates (Pollock and others, 2004). The percentage of mountain goats present within the survey frame fluctuated both diurnally and seasonally in Olympic National Park, suggesting that variations in seasonal and diurnal timing of surveys could affect trend analyses adversely unless survey boundaries are adjusted to more reliably contain the estimated population. Expanding the lower-altitude boundary as little as 100 m in altitude (that is, lowering the altitude boundary to 1,425 m) would likely reduce seasonal and temporal variation in the proportions of mountain goat locations present in the survey areas, as well as encompass a substantially greater segment of the total population (fig. 12). Defining survey boundaries on the basis of available mountain goat habitats, as in Mount Rainier and North Cascades National Park, rather than strictly on altitude, would further enhance accuracy of future counts.

Because the sample of GPS-collared mountain goats was most limited in North Cascades National Park, our understanding of altitudinal distributions of mountain goats and implications for survey design remains weakest for that park. Limited information, however, suggests population estimates may be biased low due to movements of mountain goats to lower altitudes beyond the altitude boundaries used to delimit the sampling frame for this study. Expanding the surveys to include all potential mountain goat habitats would improve the reliability of future surveys designed to estimate population abundance at the park-wide scale.

Acknowledgments

This study was funded primarily by the USGS Natural Resources Preservation Program (NRPP), although each park contributed substantial personnel and logistical support, and Washington Department of Fish and Wildlife contributed data funded from several sources (Rice and others, 2009). We could not have conducted this research without the support of each of the national park staffs including superintendents, resource managers, biologists, compliance specialists, and aviation managers. We are particularly grateful for logistical and operational support provided by Roger Christophersen and Bob Kuntz at North Cascades National Park Service Complex. We thank aviation managers Larry Nickey (Olympic), Alison Robb (Mount Rainier), and Kelly Bush (North Cascades) for their assistance in developing aviation plans and contributing to safe aerial operations in each park. We thank Matt Albright, Bill Baccus, Mike Larrabee, Rich Lechleitner, Artie Olson, and Rich Olson for managing safe helicopter operations; Dave Manson, Ellen Myers, and Roger Christophersen for serving as aerial survey observers; Dave Manson, Kim Sager, Mike Danisiewicz, Eric Penn, and Clay Parker for help with ground capture operations in Olympic National Park; Natasha Antonova for help in mapping at North Cascades National Park; John Boetsch for assistance in data management; and dispatchers at each park for assisting with radio communications during all the surveys. We appreciate the expert and safe piloting provided by Jim Pope, Jr. during aerial capture operations, Rob Olmstead and Trevor Walker during aerial helicopter surveys, and Jeff Well and John May during radio tracking flights. We thank the crew at Leading Edge Aviation for their efficient and safe animal capture services (Jim Pope, Jr., Rocky Spencer, Coburn NoEar, and Jeannie Ross, DVM). We remain grateful to our research predecessors, primarily Douglas Houston, Bruce Moorhead, Rich Olson, and Victoria Stevens, whose earlier work on mountain goats in Olympic National Park provided a foundation for this study. We would like to thank Ruth Jacobs, Shirley Koetz, and Linda Rogers for help with producing this report, and Jacqueline Olson for preparing the maps within. Layne Adams, Paul Griffin, Douglas Houston, Bob Kuntz, Mason Reid, and Victoria Stevens provided numerous helpful comments on previous drafts of this manuscript.

References Cited

Bliss, L.C., 1969, Alpine community pattern in relation to environmental parameters, *in* Greenidge, K.N.H., ed., Essays in plant geography and ecology: Halifax, Nova Scotia, Nova Scotia Museum, p. 167-184.

Burnham, K.P., and Anderson, D.R., 2002, Model selection and multimodel inference: a practical information-theoretic approach: New York, Springer-Verlag, 488 p.

Caughley, G., 1977, Analysis of vertebrate populations: New York, John Wiley and Sons.

Conover, W. J., 1980, Practical nonparametric statistics: New York, John Wiley and Sons.

D'Eon, R.G., 2003, Effects of a stationary GPS fix-rate bias on habitat-selection analyses: Journal of Wildlife Management, v. 67, no. 4, p. 858-863, accessed March 17, 2011, at http://www.jstor.org/stable/3802693.

Fonda, R.W., and Bliss, L.C., 1969, Forest vegetation of the montane and subalpine zones, Olympic Mountains, Washington: Ecological Monographs, v. 39, p. 271-301.

Franklin, J.F., and Dyrness, C.T., 1988, Natural vegetation of Oregon and Washington: Corvallis, Oregon, Oregon State University Press, 452 p.

Gitzen, R.A., Millspaugh, J.J., and Kernohan, B.J., 2006, Bandwidth selection for fixed-kernel analysis of animal utilization distributions: Journal of Wildlife Management, v. 70, p. 1334-1344.

Gonzalez-Voyer, A., Festa-Bianchet, M., and Smith, K.G., 2001, Efficiency of aerial surveys of mountain goats: Wildlife Society Bulletin, v. 29, p. 140-144.

Hamann, M.J., 1972, Vegetation of alpine and subalpine meadows of Mount Rainier National Park: Pullman Washington, Washington State University, M.S. Thesis.

Henderson, J.A., 1973, Composition, distribution and succession of subalpine meadows in Mount Rainier National Park, Washington: Corvallis, Oregon, Oregon State University, Ph.D. Dissertation.

Horne, J.S., and Garton, E.O., 2006, Likelihood cross-validation versus least squares cross-validation for choosing the smoothing parameter in kernel home-range analysis: Journal of Wildlife Management, v. 70, no. 3, p. 641-648, doi: 10.2193/0022-541X(2006)70[641:LCVLSC]2.0.CO;2, accessed March 17, 2011, at http://www.bioone.org/doi/full/10.2193/0022-541X%282006%2970%5B641%3ALCVLSC%5D2.0.CO%3B2.

Hosmer, D.W., and Lemeshow, S., 2000, Applied Logistic Regression, Second Edition: New York, John Wiley and Sons.

Houston, D.B., Moorhead, B.B., and Olson, R.W., 1986, An aerial census of mountain goats in the Olympic Mountain Range, Washington: Northwest Science, v. 60, p. 131-136.

Houston, D.G., Moorhead B.B., and Olson, R.W., 1991, Mountain goat population trends in the Olympic Mountain Range, Washington: Northwest Science v. 65, p. 212-216.

Houston, D.B., Olson, R.W., Hoffman, R.A., and Moorhead, B.B., 1994b, Mountain goat census in the Olympic Mountains Range, July 1994, Olympic National Park: Report to the Superintendent, Port Angeles, Washington, Olympic National Park.

Houston, D.B., Schreiner, E.G., and Moorhead, B.B., 1994a, Mountain goats in Olympic National Park: biology and management of an introduced species: Port Angeles, Washington, National Park Service, Scientific Monograph NPS/NROLYM/NRSM-94/25.

Kuromoto, R.T., and Bliss, L.C., 1970, Ecology of subalpine meadows in the Olympic Mountains, Washington: Ecological Monographs, v. 40, p. 317-347.

Laver, P.N., and Kelly, M.J., 2008, A critical review of home range studies: Journal of Wildlife Management, v. 72, p. 290-298.

National Park Service, 1995, Goats in Olympic National Park, Draft environmental impact statement for mountain goat management: Port Angeles, Washington, Olympic National Park.

Noss, R.F., Graham, R., McCullough, D.R., Ramsey, F.L., Seavey, J., Whitlock, C., and Williams, M.P., 2000, Review of scientific material relevant to the occurrence, ecosystem role, and test management options for mountain goats in Olympic National Park: Conservation Biology Institute, Corvallis, Oregon, accessed April 9, 2011, at http://consbio.org/what-we-do/review-of-scientific-material-relevant-to-the/download.

Olson, R.W., 1994, Appendix C. Mountain Goat Capture, in Houston, D.B., Schreiner, E.G., and Moorhead, B.B., eds., Mountain goats in Olympic National Park: biology and management of an introduced species, Scientific Monograph NPS/NROLYM/NRSM-94/25: Port Angeles, Washington, National Park Service, p. 294-295.

Pollock, K.H., Marsh, H., Bailey, L.L., Farnsworth, G.L., Simons, T.R., and Alldredge, M.W., 2004, Separating components of detection probability in abundance estimations: an overview with diverse examples, in Thompson, W.L., ed., Sampling rare or elusive species: Washington D.C., Island Press, p. 43-58.

Rice, C.G., 2008, Seasonal altitudinal movements of mountain goats: Journal of Wildlife Management: v. 72, no. 8, p. 1706-1716, doi:10.2193/2007-584, accessed March 17, 2011, at http://www.bioone.org/doi/abs/10.2193/2007-584.

Rice, C.G., and Gay, D., 2010, Effects of mountain goat harvest on historic and contemporary populations: Northwestern Naturalist, v. 91, p. 40-57.

Rice, C.G., Jenkins, K.J., and Chang, W.Y., 2009, A sightability model for mountain goats: Journal of Wildlife Management, v. 73, no. 3, p. 468-478, doi:10.2193/2008-196, accessed March 17, 2011, at http://www.bioone.org/doi/abs/10.2193/2008-196.

Rodgers, A.R., Carr, A.P., Smith, L., and Kie, J.G., 2005, HRT: Home Range Tools for ArcGIS: Thunder Bay, Ontario, Canada, Ontario Ministry of Natural Resources, Centre for Northern Forest Ecosystem Research.

Sager-Fradkin, K.A., Jenkins, K.J., Hoffman, R.A., Happe, P.J., Beecham, J.J., and Wright, R.G., 2007, Fix success and accuracy of global positioning system collars in old-growth temperate coniferous forests: Journal of Wildlife Management, v. 71, no. 4, p. 1298-1308, doi: 10.2193/2006-367, accessed March 17, 2011, at http://www.bioone.org/doi/abs/10.2193/2006-367.

Samuel, M.D., Garton, E.O., Schlegel, M.W., and Carson, R.G., 1987, Visibility bias during aerial surveys of elk in north-central Idaho: Journal of Wildlife Management, v. 51, no. 3, p. 622-630, accessed March 17, 2011, at http://www.jstor.org/stable/3801280.

Schwartz, C.C., Podruzny, S., Cain, S.L., and Cherry, S., 2009, Performance of spread spectrum global positioning system collars on grizzly and black bears: Journal of Wildlife Management, v. 73, no. 7, p. 1174-1183, doi:10.2193/2008-514, accessed March 17, 2011, at http://www.bioone.org/doi/full/10.2193/2008-514.

Stevens, V., 1979, Mountain goat (*Oreamnos americanus*) habitat utilization in Olympic National Park: University of Washington, Seattle, M.S. thesis, 106 p.

Udevitz, M.S., Shults, B.S., Adams, L.G., and Kleckner, C., 2006, Evaluation of aerial survey methods for Dall's Sheep: Wildlife Society Bulletin, v. 34, p. 732-740.

Wells, A., 2006, Global position system (GPS) bias correction and habitat analysis of mountain goats (*Oreamnos americanus*) in the Cascades of Washington State, USA: Bellingham, Washington, Western Washington University, M.S. Thesis.

Worton, B.J., 1989, Kernel methods for estimating the utilization distribution in home-range studies: Ecology, v. 70, p. 164-168.

Zar, J.H., 1984, Biostatistical analysis: Second Edition, Englewood Cliffs, New Jersey, Prentice-Hall Inc.

Appendix 1. Drug induction times, vital signs, and physical measurements of 20 mountain goats captured in Mount Rainier, North Cascades, and Olympic National Parks, Washington, 2005–07.

[Data are provided only for goats captured by NPS and USGS crews and contractors. Data are not provided for five mountain goats captured by WDFW crews. Drug induction time: carfentanil, minutes elapsed between the time of injection with 2.4 mg carfentanil citrate and the time the animal was recorded down in a recumbent position; naltrexone, minutes elapsed between the time of injection with 400 mg naltrexone hydrochloride and the time the animal was recorded standing. min, minutes; Temp, temperature; Resp., respiration; °F, degrees Fahrenheit; cm, centimeter; circumf., circumference; F, female; M, male; NR, not recorded; NA, not applicable]

Collar ID	Sex	Lactating	Drug induction time (min)		Vital signs			Horth length (cm)		Body measurements (cm)		
			Carfentanil	Naltrexone	Temp. (°F)	Resp. (min^{-1})	Pulse (min^{-1})	Left	Right	Chest circumf.	Total length	Neck circumf.
					Mount Rainier National Park							
876	F	NR	4	2	101.4	16	96	20.0	20.5	107.0	135.0	45.0
881	F	Yes	5	3	103.3	16	132	20.5	21.5	98.5		44.0
1894	M	NA	6	3	102.6			22.5	23.0			55.0
1900	F	NR	4	3	102.7	24	148	21.0	22.0	125.0	137.5	49.5
1903	F	Yes	4	3	104.2	16	100	18.5	18.0	109.0	128.5	40.0
917-2	M	NA			102.4			21.8	22.3			
					North Cascades National Park							
889	M	NA	3	2	101.7	20	150	20.0	21.0	135.0	180.0	54.0
1895	F	Yes	3	4	102.7			21.0	21.5	114.5	152.5	43.5
1897	F	No	4	3	103.1			22.0	21.5	97.0	139.5	41.5
1901	F	Yes	4	4	103.0			22.0	21.0	99.0	138.5	39.0
					Olympic National Park							
877	F	Yes	3	2	101.7	20	100	21.0	20.6	126.0	[1]67.0	45.0
882	F	Yes						23.0		121.0		40.0
883	M	NA		3	102.7	20		23.0	21.5	151.0	175.0	57.0
884	F	No						18.2	20.0	101.0	149.0	38.0
885	F	Yes	6		103.5	20	84	21.5	21.5	114.0	144.0	45.0
1891	M	NA	3	3	102.0	16		20.5	18.5	142.0	174.0	55.0
1892	F	NR	2		103.0	16	120					
1898	M	NA	5		102.5	24	64	22.0	22.0	140.0	158.0	55.5
1899	F	Yes	4	5	100.5	16		24.0	24.0	116.0	153.0	43.0
1902	F	Yes	4	3	102.6	15		21.5	22.0	107.0	140.5	42.0

[1]Suspected recording error in the field.

Appendix 2.   Seasonal adaptive kernel home range (95-percent utilization distribution) and core area (50-percent UD) estimates of individual GPS-collared mountain goats in Mount Rainier, North Cascades, and Olympic National Parks, Washington, 2003–08.

[GPS, Global Positioning System; UD, utilization distribution; km², square kilometers]

Collar identification No.	Summer ranges (km²)			Winter ranges (km²)		
	Number of GPS locations	95-percent UD	50-percent UD	Number of GPS locations	95-percent UD	50-percent UD
FEMALE						
Mount Rainier National Park						
550	543	8.62	0.92	811	1.25	0.12
876	941	7.10	0.85	2,459	6.96	0.47
881	59	6.70	0.82	505	1.45	0.25
911	828	8.24	0.73	1,034	9.46	0.83
1900	57	6.24	1.33	215	1.77	0.25
1903	672	6.04	0.63	597	5.32	0.58
North Cascades National Park						
541	2,127	4.51	0.90	2,709	2.79	0.38
1895	386	9.96	1.13	345	3.53	0.45
1901	988	10.77	1.99	437	3.78	0.60
Olympic National Park						
882	1,486	6.31	0.74	2,020	2.79	0.24
884	947	7.72	1.15	1,720	2.59	0.44
885	938	7.05	0.94	1,133	2.73	0.25
1892	1,803	16.41	1.22	1,848	0.87	0.07
1899	596	2.86	0.45	750	0.68	0.07
1902	174	6.63	0.51	261	1.71	0.17
MALE						
Mount Rainer National Park						
936	2,234	37.03	2.68	1,794	4.50	0.28
1894	347	2.79	0.54	850	7.51	0.57
917-2	346	2.61	0.20			
North Cascades National Park						
889	907	15.00	1.96	405	6.90	0.53
Olympic National Park						
883	1,340	8.19	0.29	877	4.63	0.35
1891	199	1.63	0.16	98	3.58	0.56
1898	1,037	7.74	0.37	1,422	5.80	0.31
1899-2	1,107	3.64	0.62	1,260	5.21	0.50

Appendix 3.   Maps showing seasonal distributions of selected GPS-collared mountain goats in Mount Rainier, North Cascades, and Olympic National Parks, Washington, 2003–07. 95-, 80-, and 50-percent adaptive kernel utilization distributions are shown for individual mountain goats.

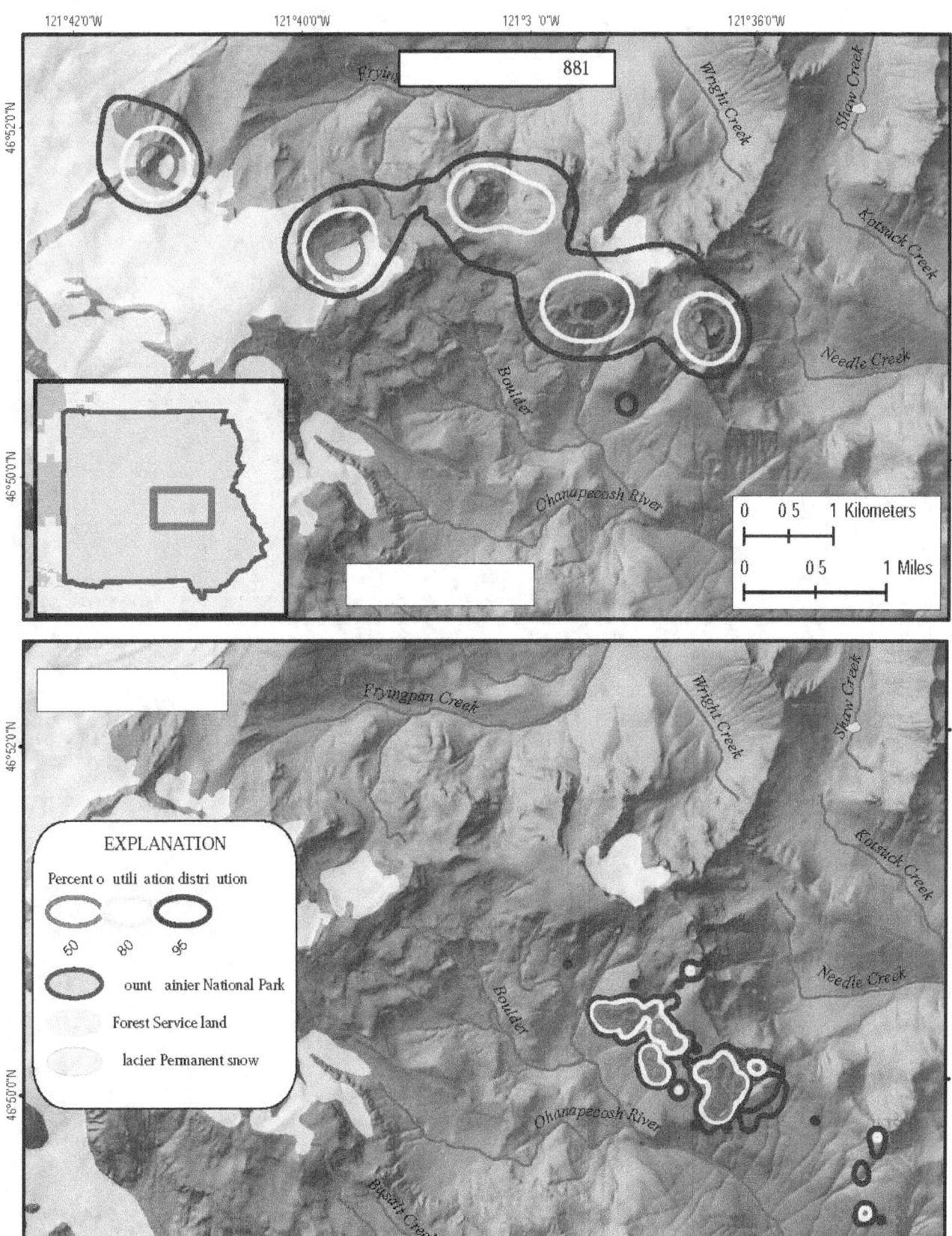

Appendix 3.   Maps showing seasonal distributions of selected GPS-collared mountain goats in Mount Rainier, North Cascades, and Olympic National Parks, Washington, 2003–07.—Continued. 95-, 80-, and 50-percent adaptive kernel utilization distributions are shown for individual mountain goats.

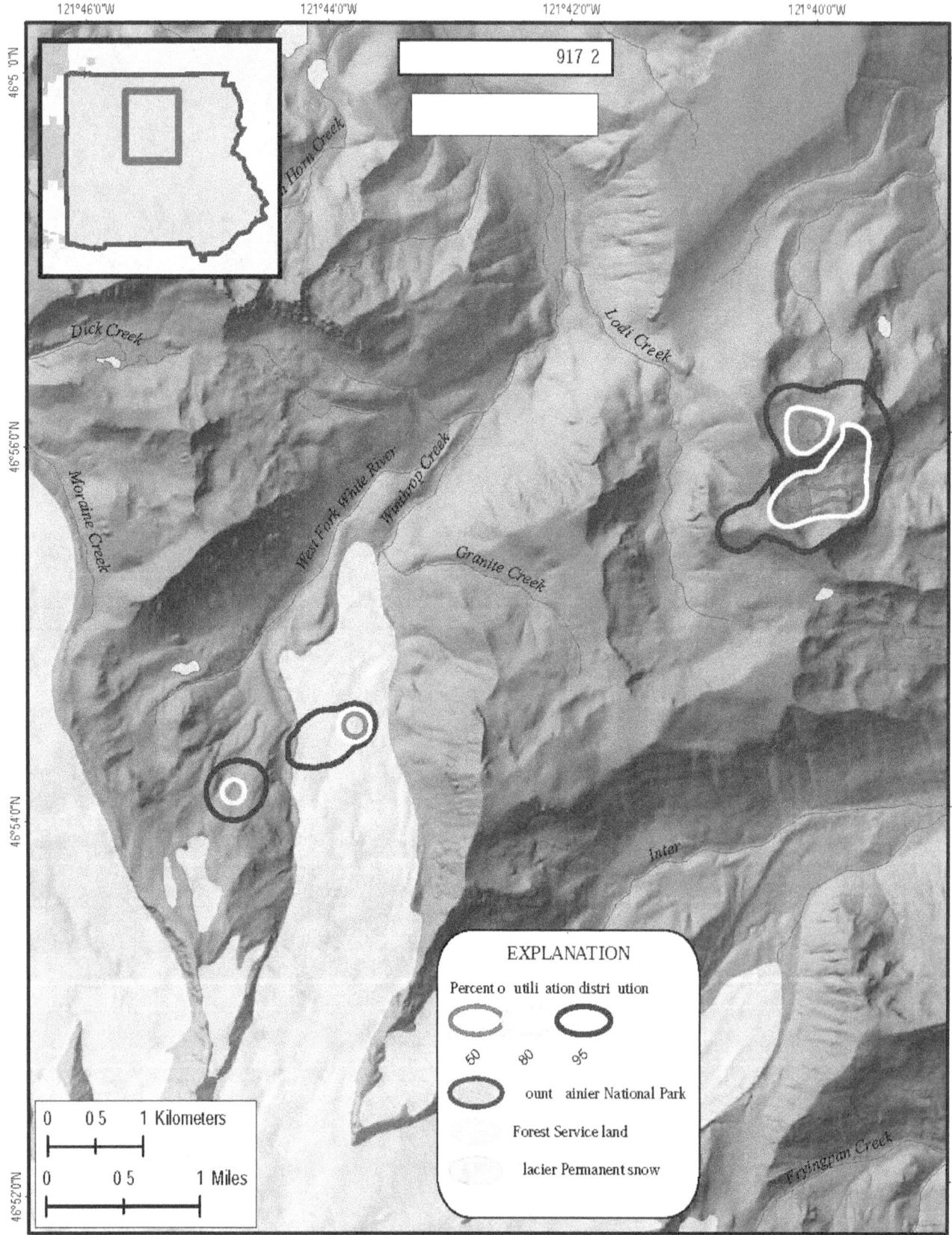

Appendix 3.   Maps showing seasonal distributions of selected GPS-collared mountain goats in Mount Rainier, North Cascades, and Olympic National Parks, Washington, 2003–07.—Continued. 95-, 80-, and 50-percent adaptive kernel utilization distributions are shown for individual mountain goats.

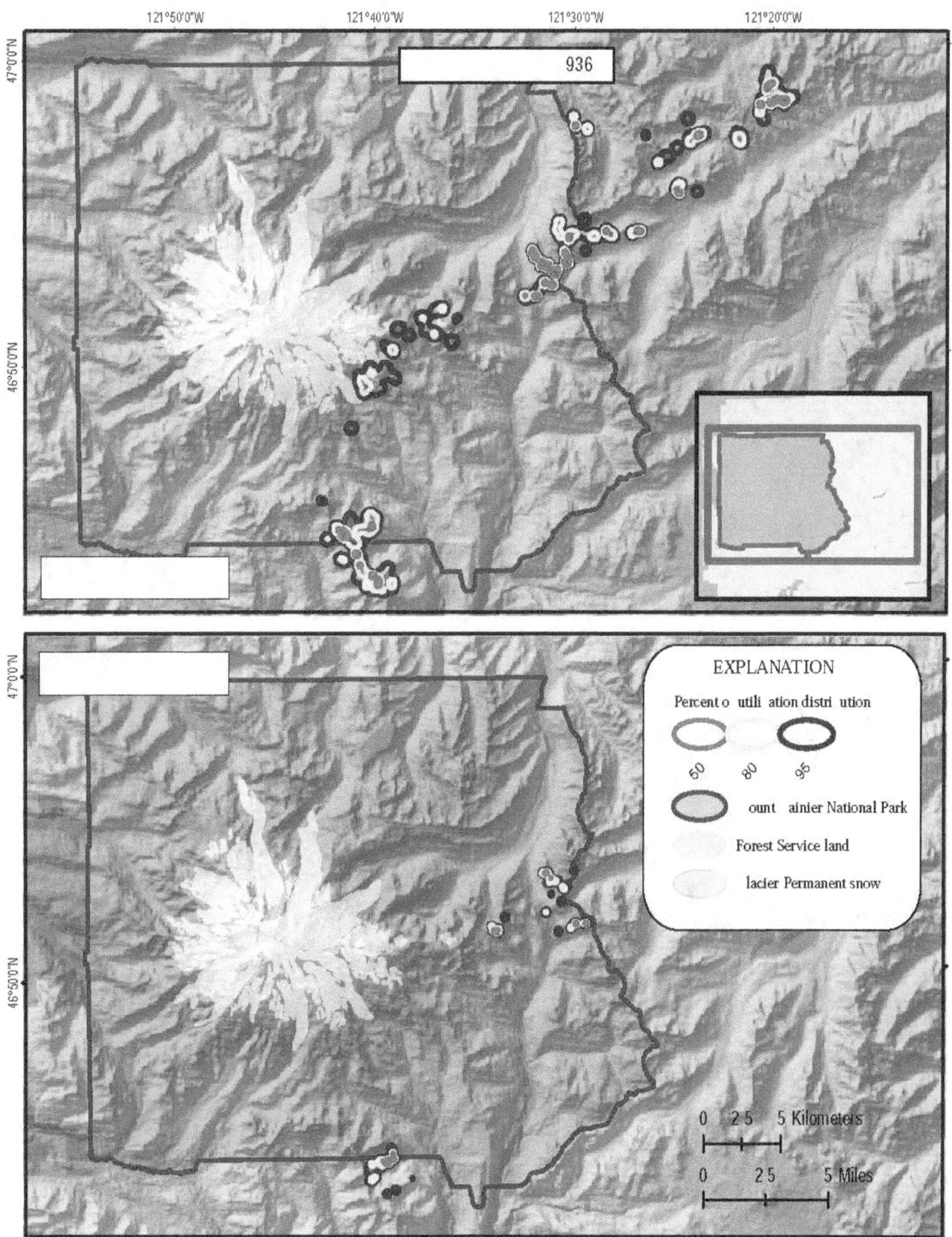

Appendix 3.   Maps showing seasonal distributions of selected GPS-collared mountain goats in Mount Rainier, North Cascades, and Olympic National Parks, Washington, 2003–07.—Continued. 95-, 80-, and 50-percent adaptive kernel utilization distributions are shown for individual mountain goats.

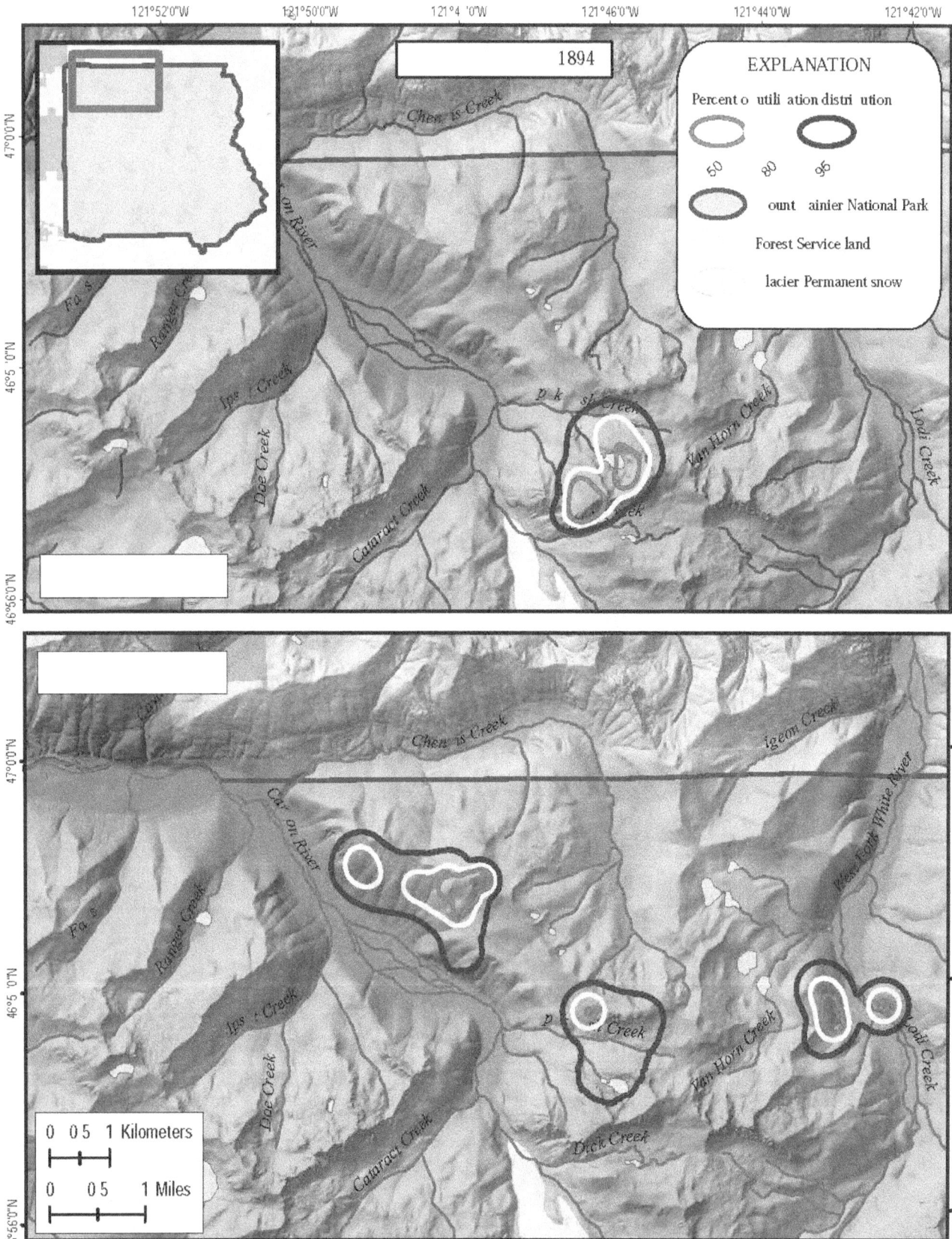

Appendix 3. Maps showing seasonal distributions of selected GPS-collared mountain goats in Mount Rainier, North Cascades, and Olympic National Parks, Washington, 2003–07.—Continued. 95-, 80-, and 50-percent adaptive kernel utilization distributions are shown for individual mountain goats.

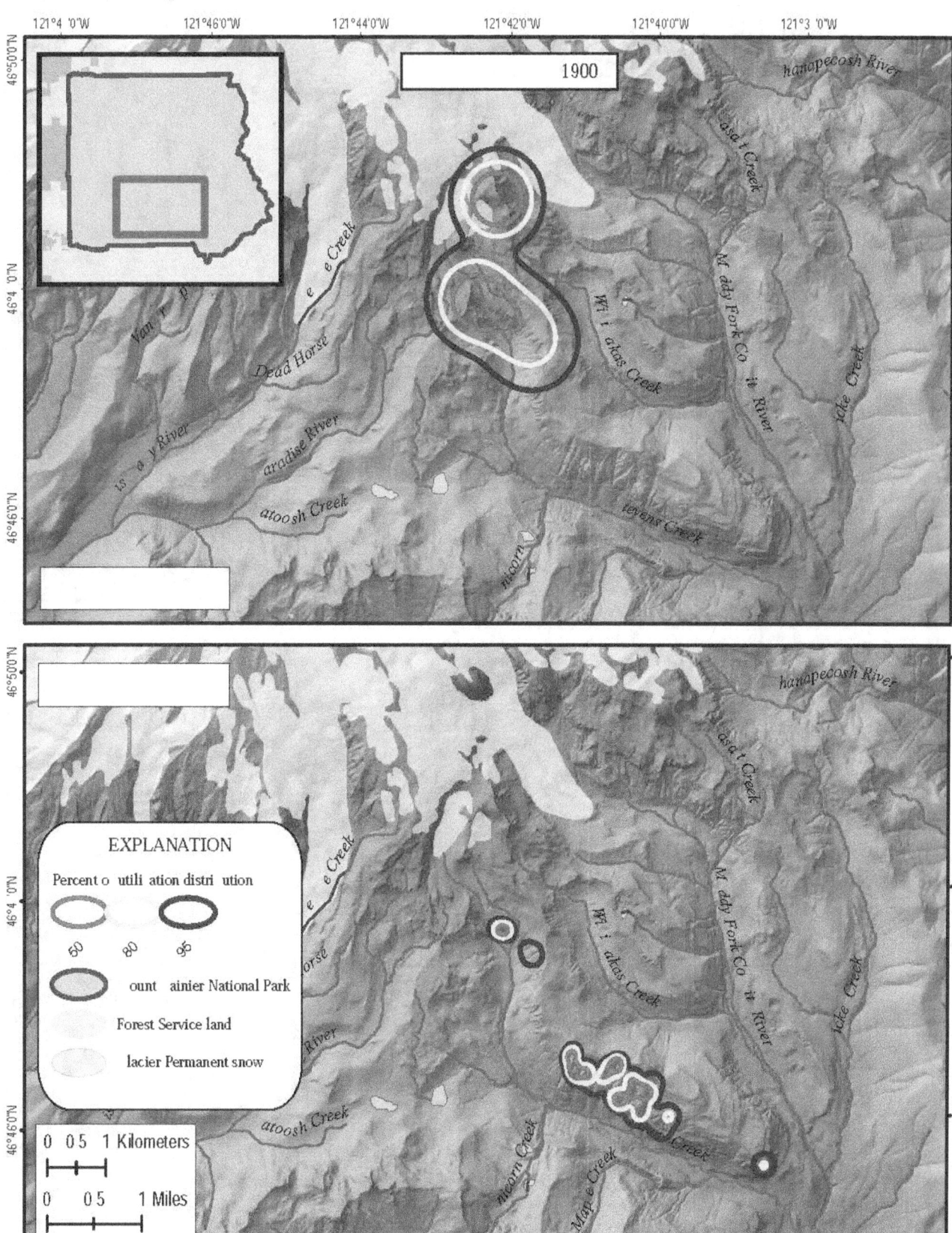

Appendix 3.   Maps showing seasonal distributions of selected GPS-collared mountain goats in Mount Rainier, North Cascades, and Olympic National Parks, Washington, 2003–07.—Continued. 95-, 80-, and 50-percent adaptive kernel utilization distributions are shown for individual mountain goats.

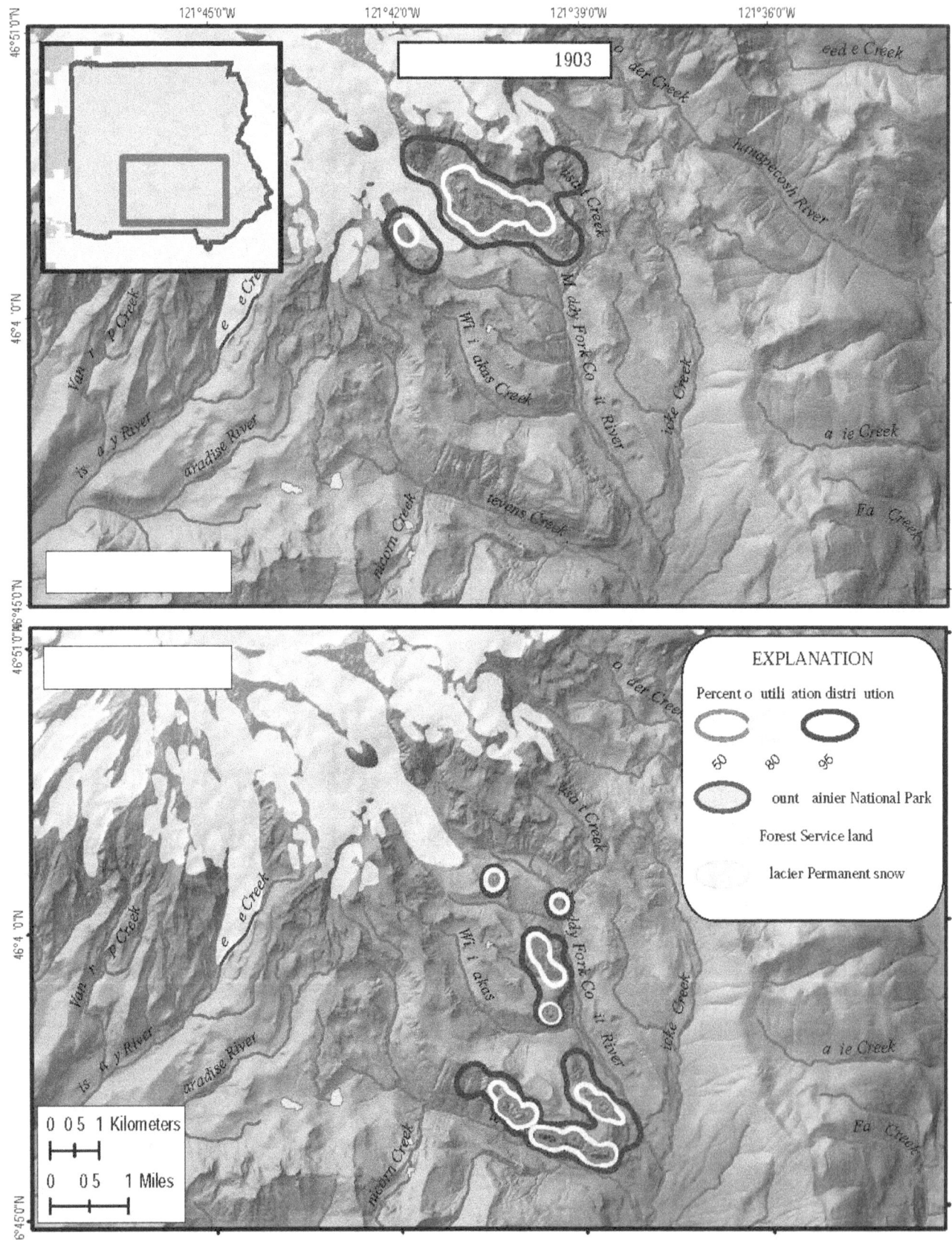

Appendix 3.   Maps showing seasonal distributions of selected GPS-collared mountain goats in Mount Rainier, North Cascades, and Olympic National Parks, Washington, 2003–07.—Continued. 95-, 80-, and 50-percent adaptive kernel utilization distributions are shown for individual mountain goats.

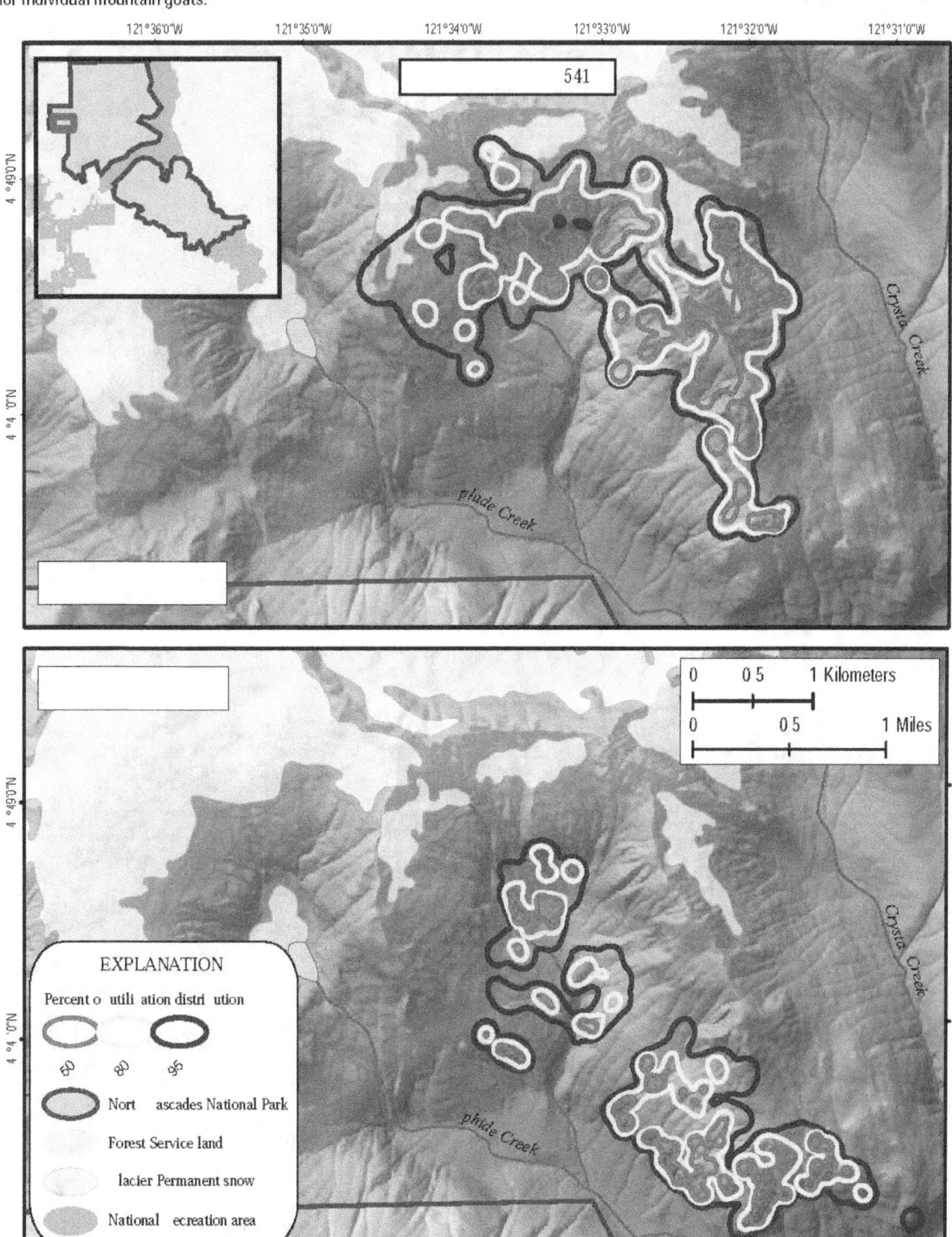

Appendix 3.   Maps showing seasonal distributions of selected GPS-collared mountain goats in Mount Rainier, North Cascades, and Olympic National Parks, Washington, 2003–07.—Continued. 95-, 80-, and 50-percent adaptive kernel utilization distributions are shown for individual mountain goats.

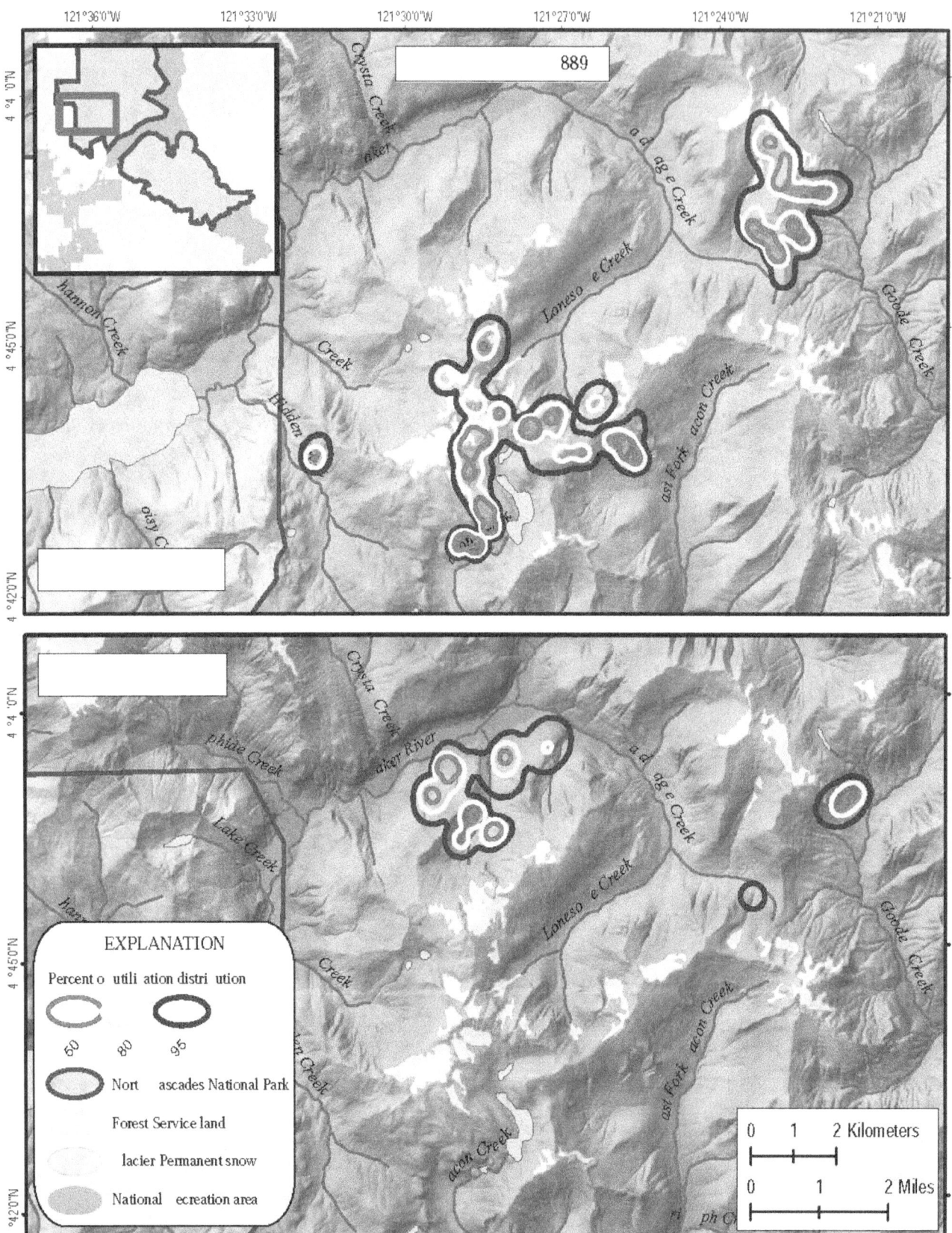

Appendix 3.   Maps showing seasonal distributions of selected GPS-collared mountain goats in Mount Rainier, North Cascades, and Olympic National Parks, Washington, 2003–07.—Continued. 95-, 80-, and 50-percent adaptive kernel utilization distributions are shown for individual mountain goats.

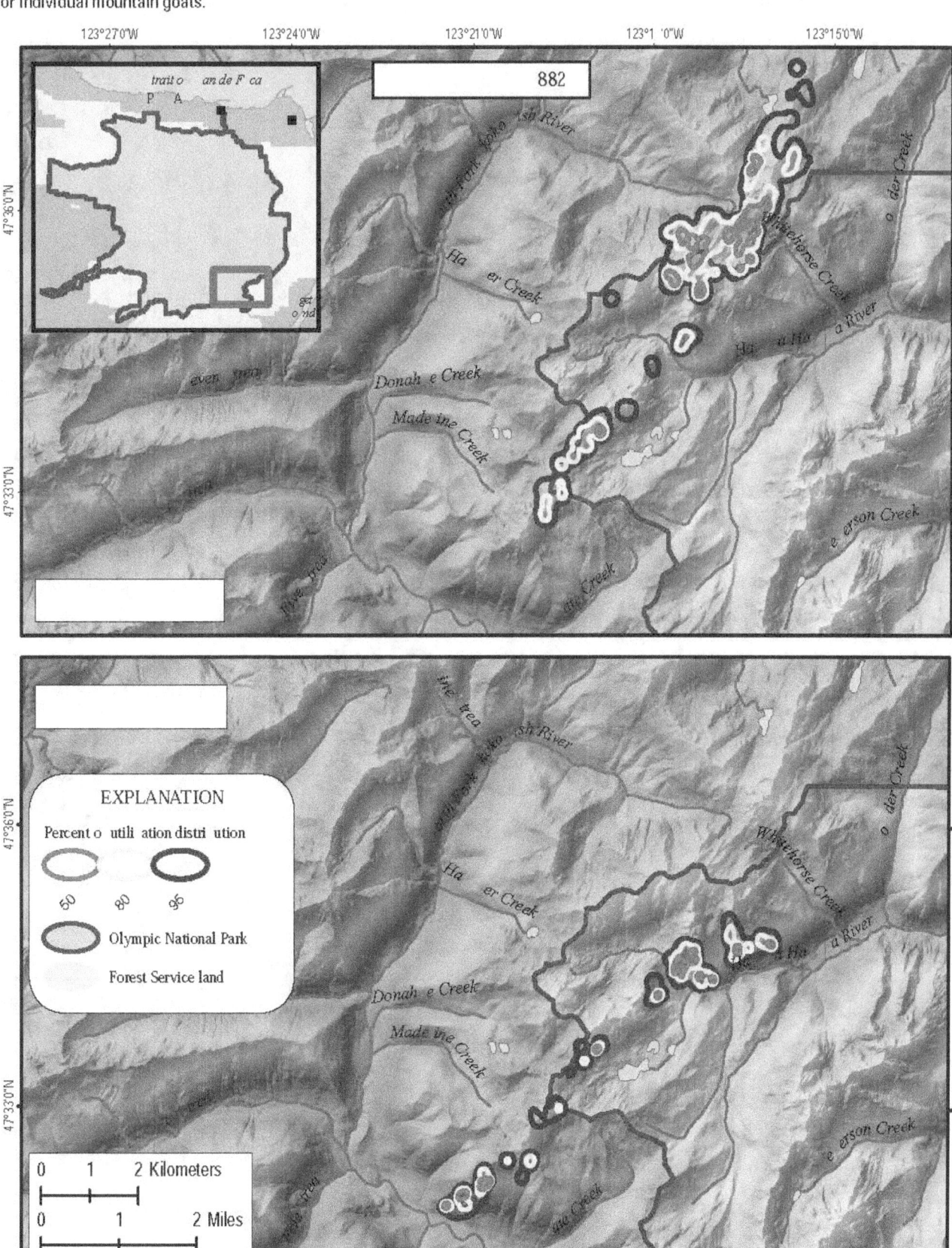

Appendix 3.   Maps showing seasonal distributions of selected GPS-collared mountain goats in Mount Rainier, North Cascades, and Olympic National Parks, Washington, 2003–07.—Continued. 95-, 80-, and 50-percent adaptive kernel utilization distributions are shown for individual mountain goats.

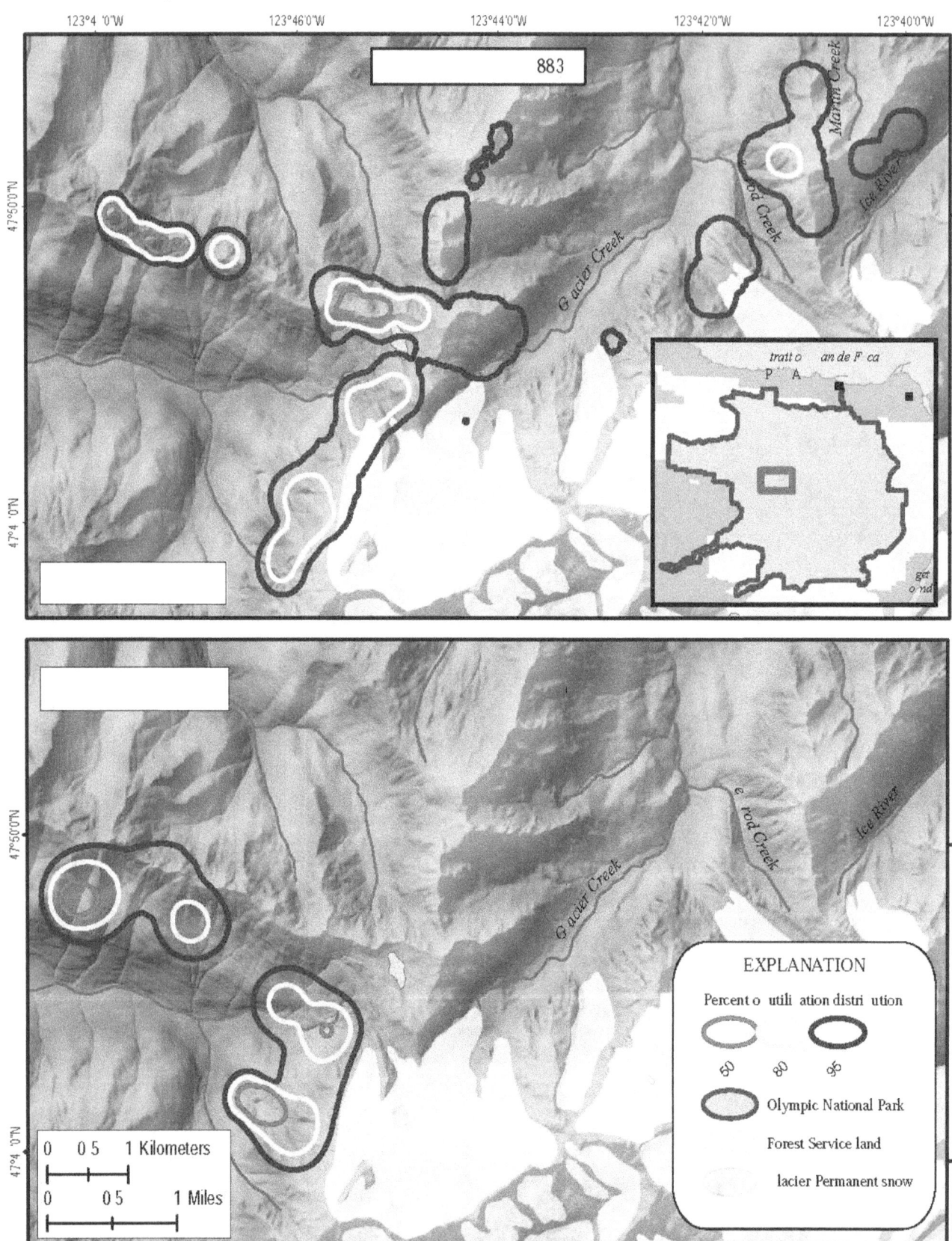

Appendix 3.   Maps showing seasonal distributions of selected GPS-collared mountain goats in Mount Rainier, North Cascades, and Olympic National Parks, Washington, 2003–07.—Continued. 95-, 80-, and 50-percent adaptive kernel utilization distributions are shown for individual mountain goats.

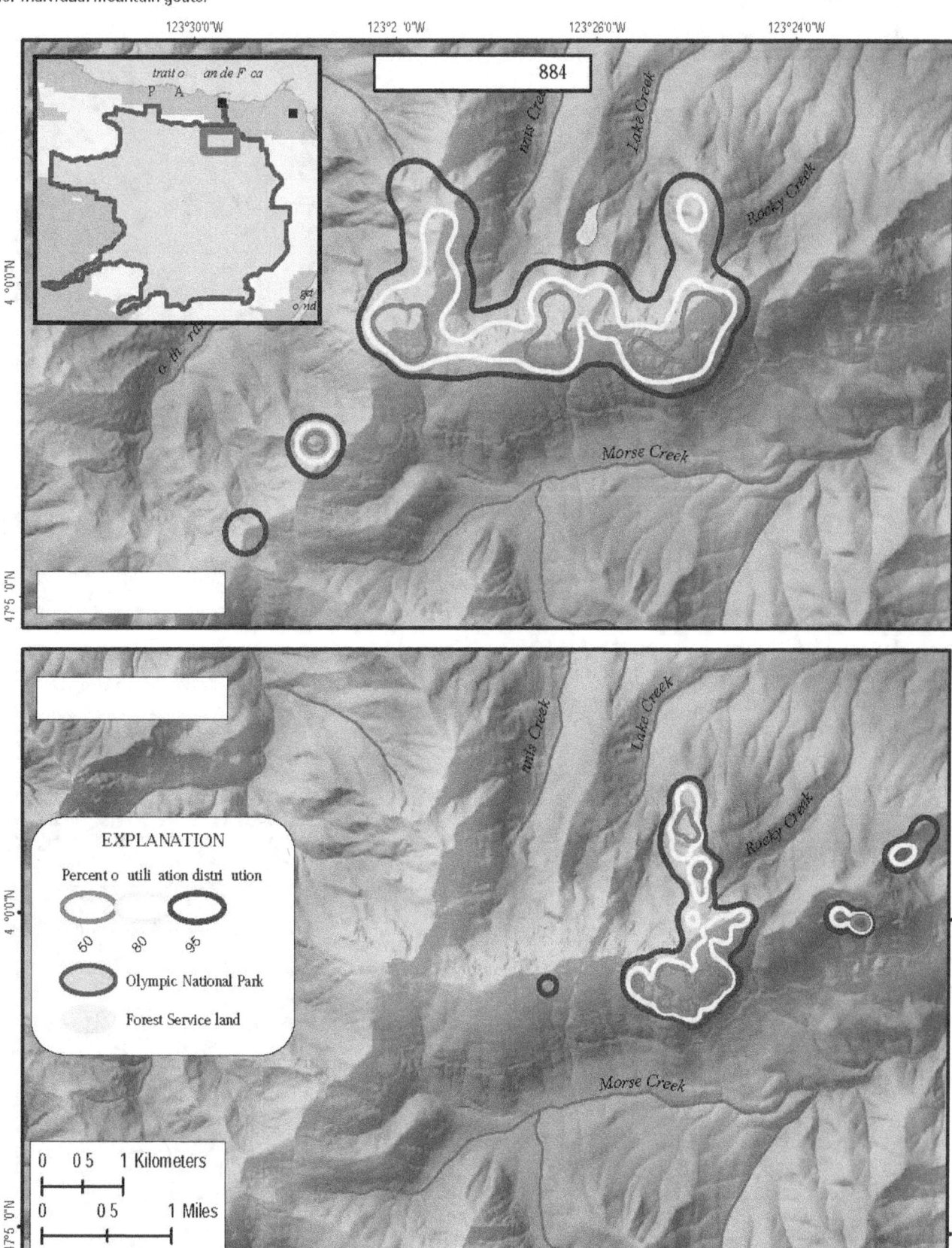

Appendix 3.   Maps showing seasonal distributions of selected GPS-collared mountain goats in Mount Rainier, North Cascades, and Olympic National Parks, Washington, 2003–07.—Continued. 95-, 80-, and 50-percent adaptive kernel utilization distributions are shown for individual mountain goats.

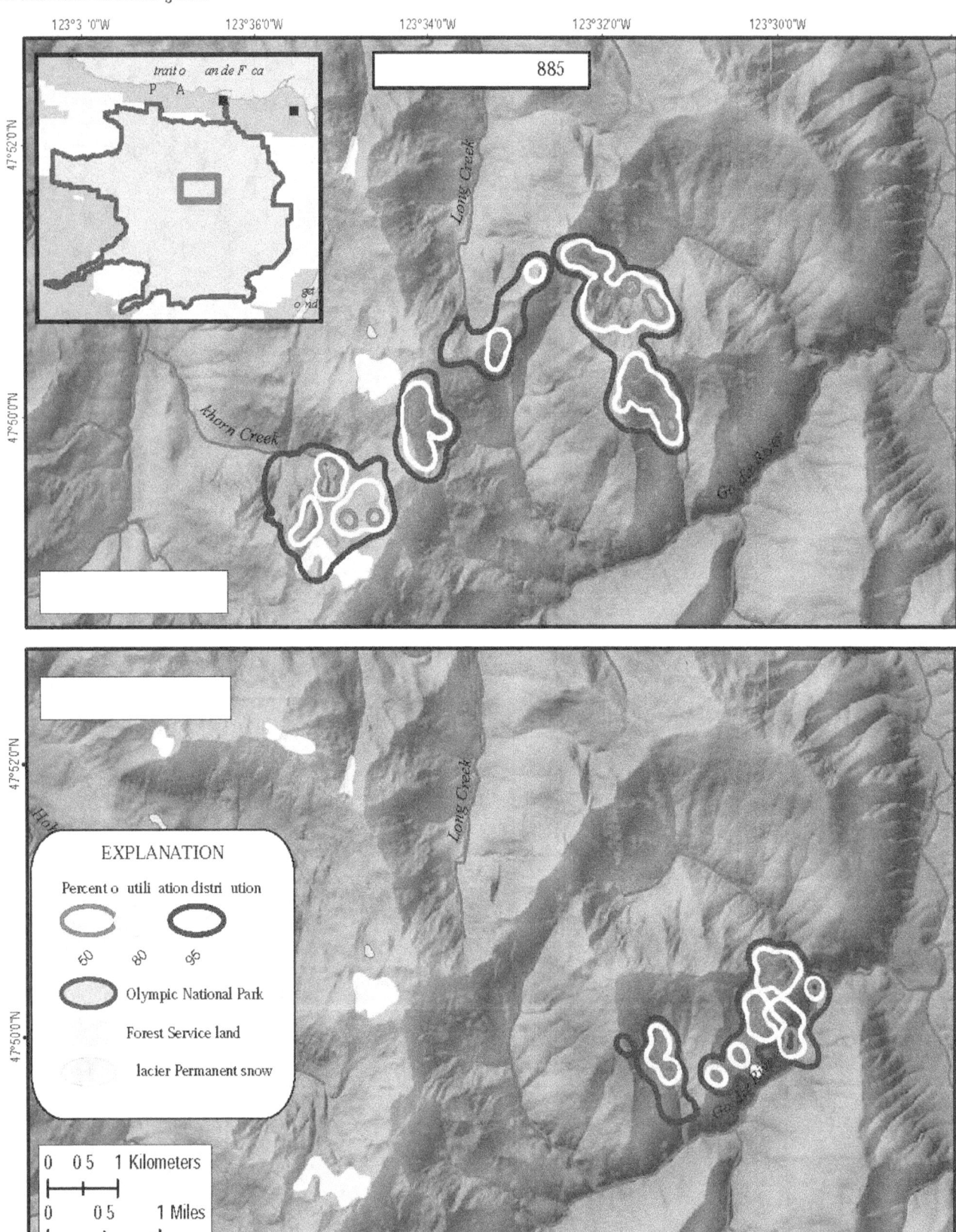

Appendix 3. Maps showing seasonal distributions of selected GPS-collared mountain goats in Mount Rainier, North Cascades, and Olympic National Parks, Washington, 2003–07.—Continued. 95-, 80-, and 50-percent adaptive kernel utilization distributions are shown for individual mountain goats.

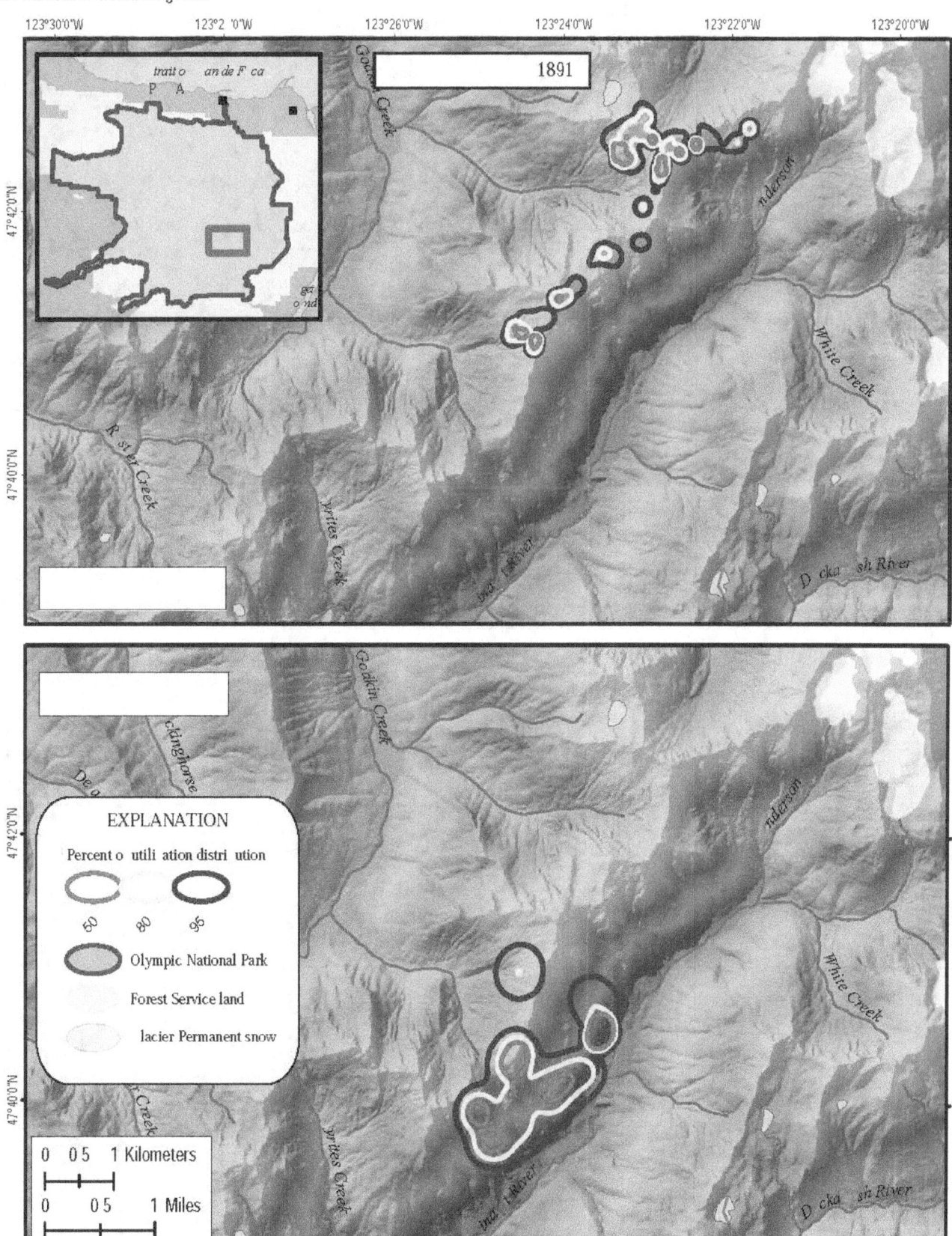

Appendix 3.   Maps showing seasonal distributions of selected GPS-collared mountain goats in Mount Rainier, North Cascades, and Olympic National Parks, Washington, 2003–07.—Continued. 95-, 80-, and 50-percent adaptive kernel utilization distributions are shown for individual mountain goats.

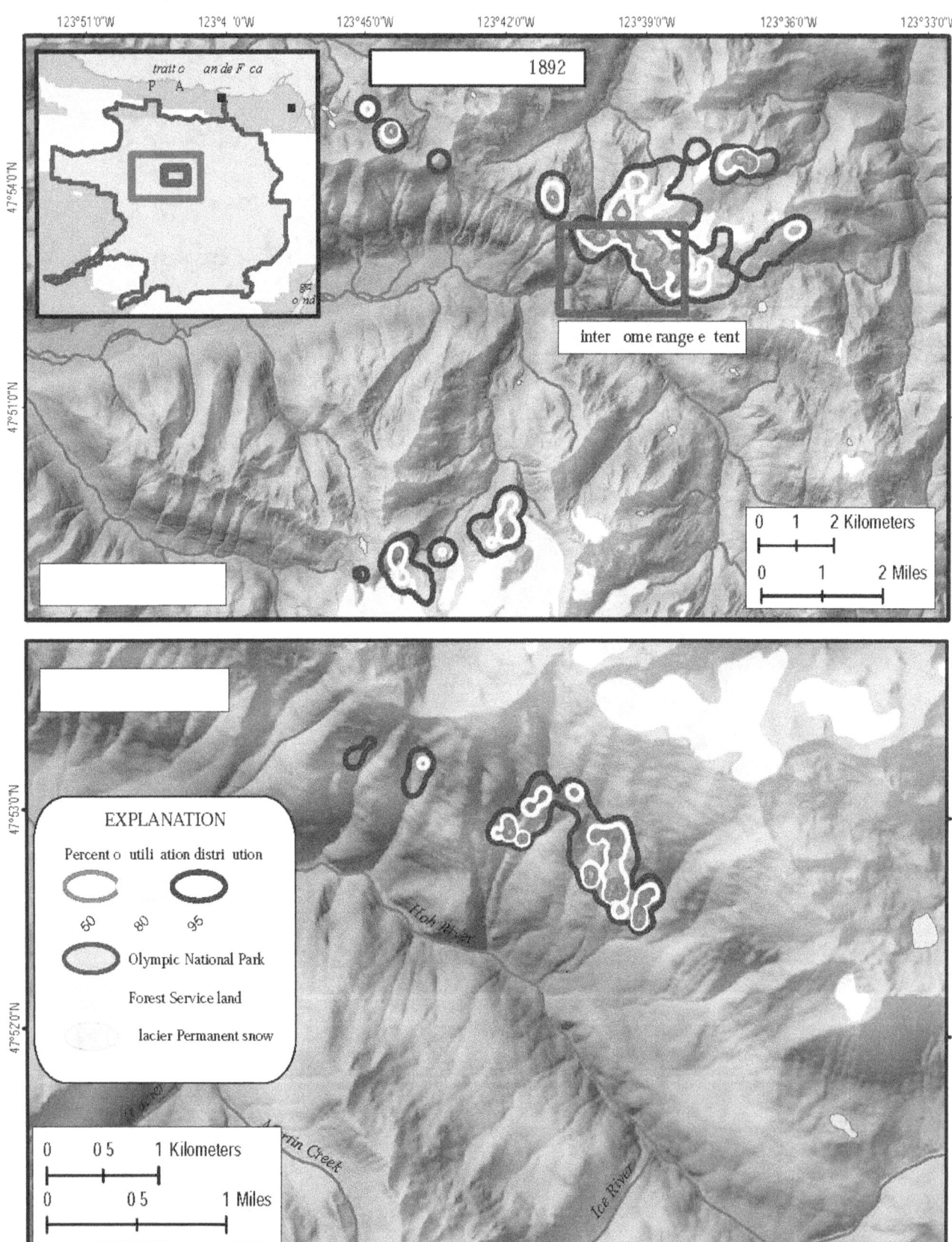

Appendix 3.   Maps showing seasonal distributions of selected GPS-collared mountain goats in Mount Rainier, North Cascades, and Olympic National Parks, Washington, 2003–07.—Continued. 95-, 80-, and 50-percent adaptive kernel utilization distributions are shown for individual mountain goats.

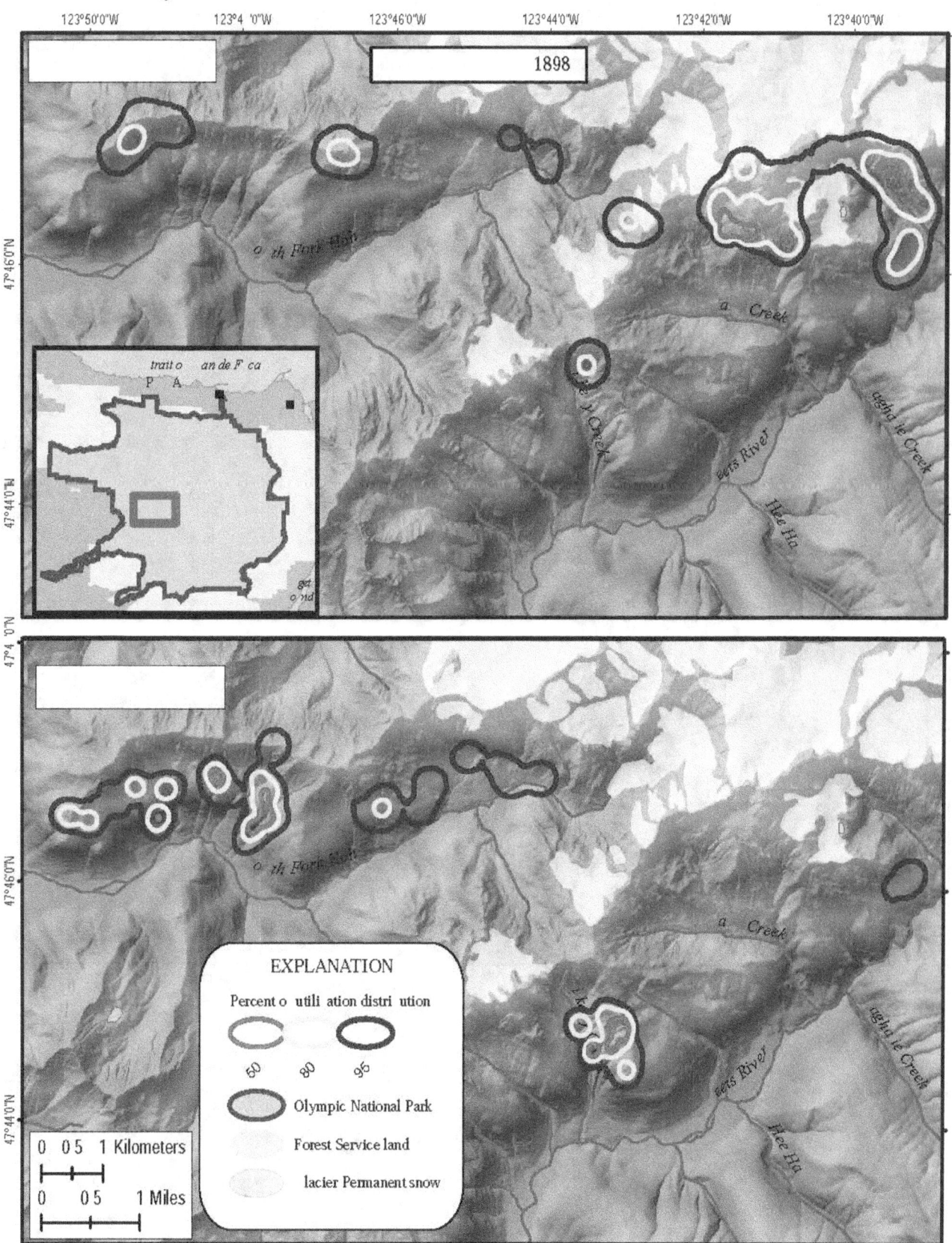

Appendix 3.   Maps showing seasonal distributions of selected GPS-collared mountain goats in Mount Rainier, North Cascades, and Olympic National Parks, Washington, 2003–07.—Continued. 95-, 80-, and 50-percent adaptive kernel utilization distributions are shown for individual mountain goats.

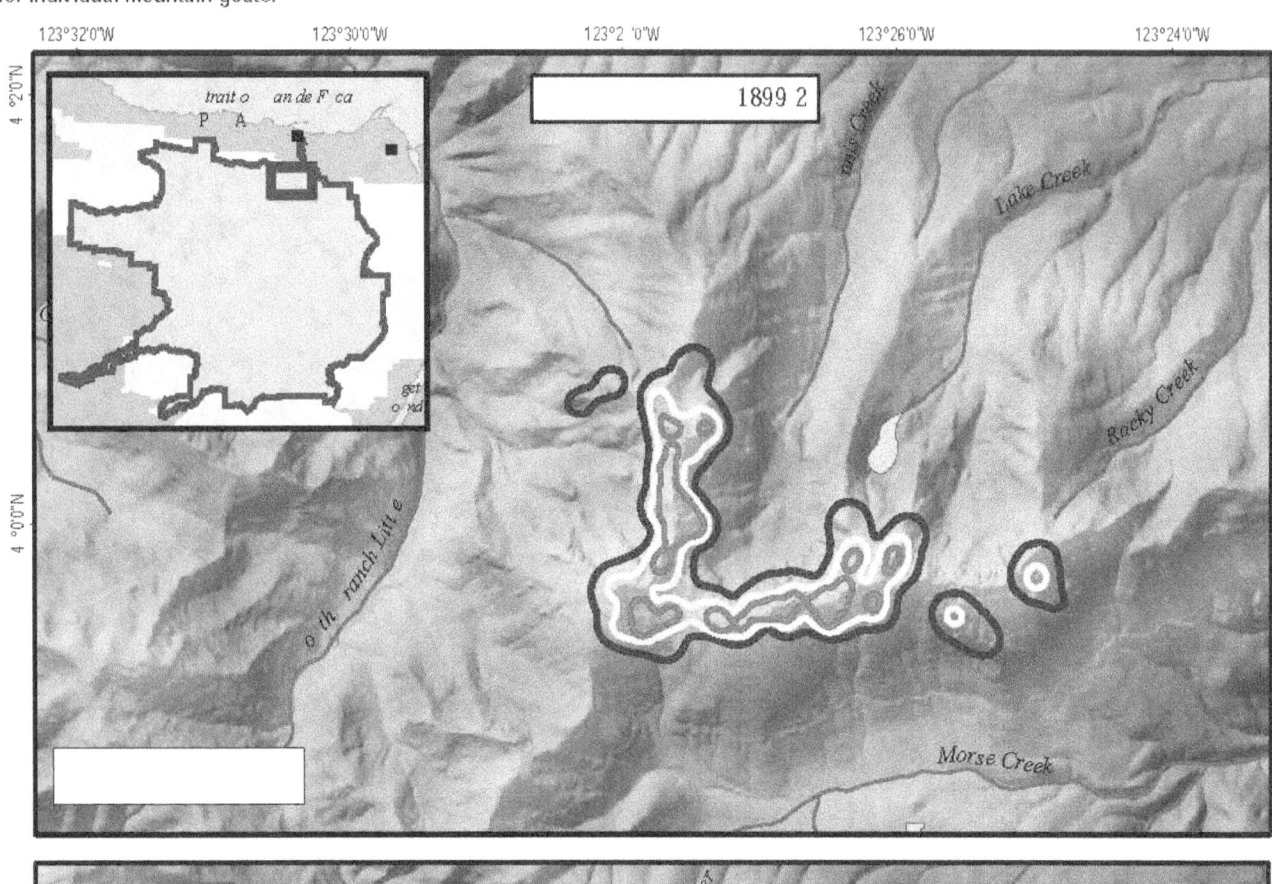

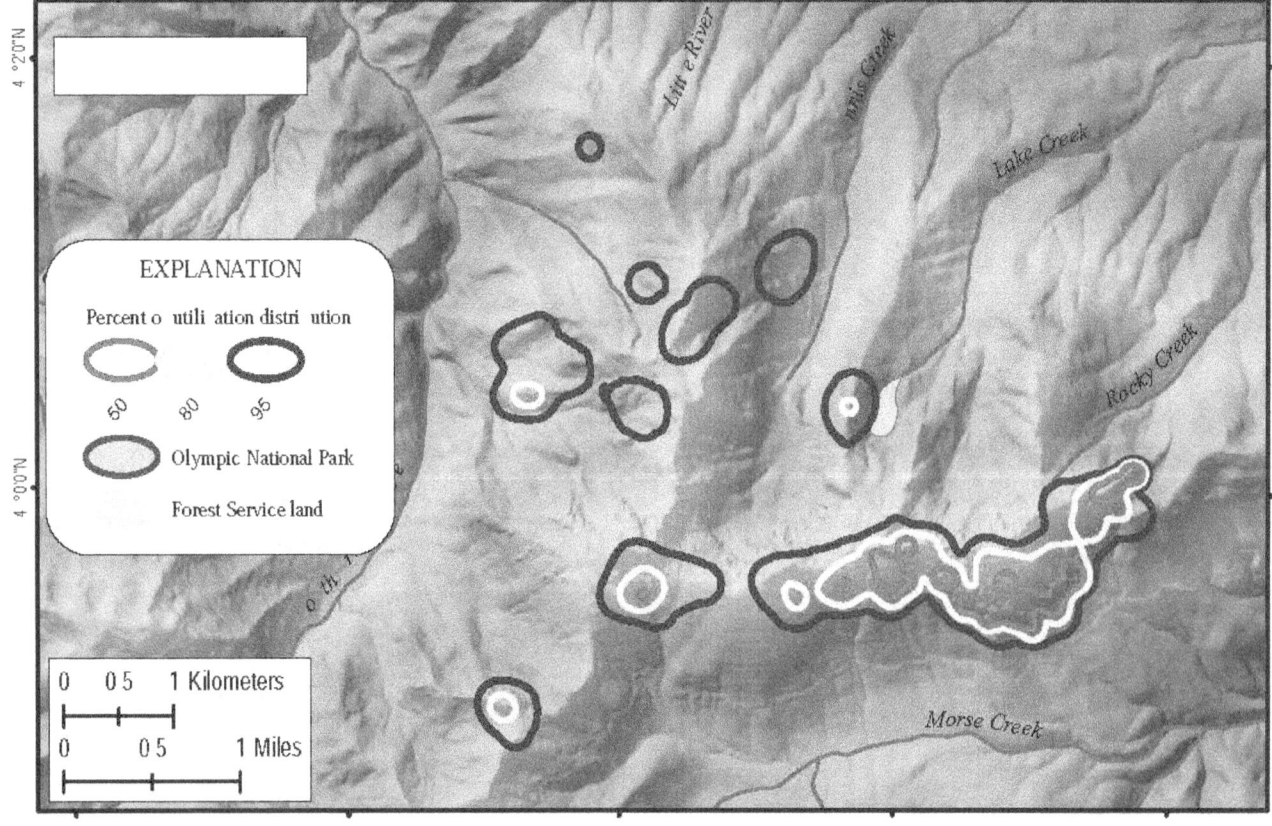

Appendix 3.   Maps showing seasonal distributions of selected GPS-collared mountain goats in Mount Rainier, North Cascades, and Olympic National Parks, Washington, 2003–07.—Continued. 95-, 80-, and 50-percent adaptive kernel utilization distributions are shown for individual mountain goats.

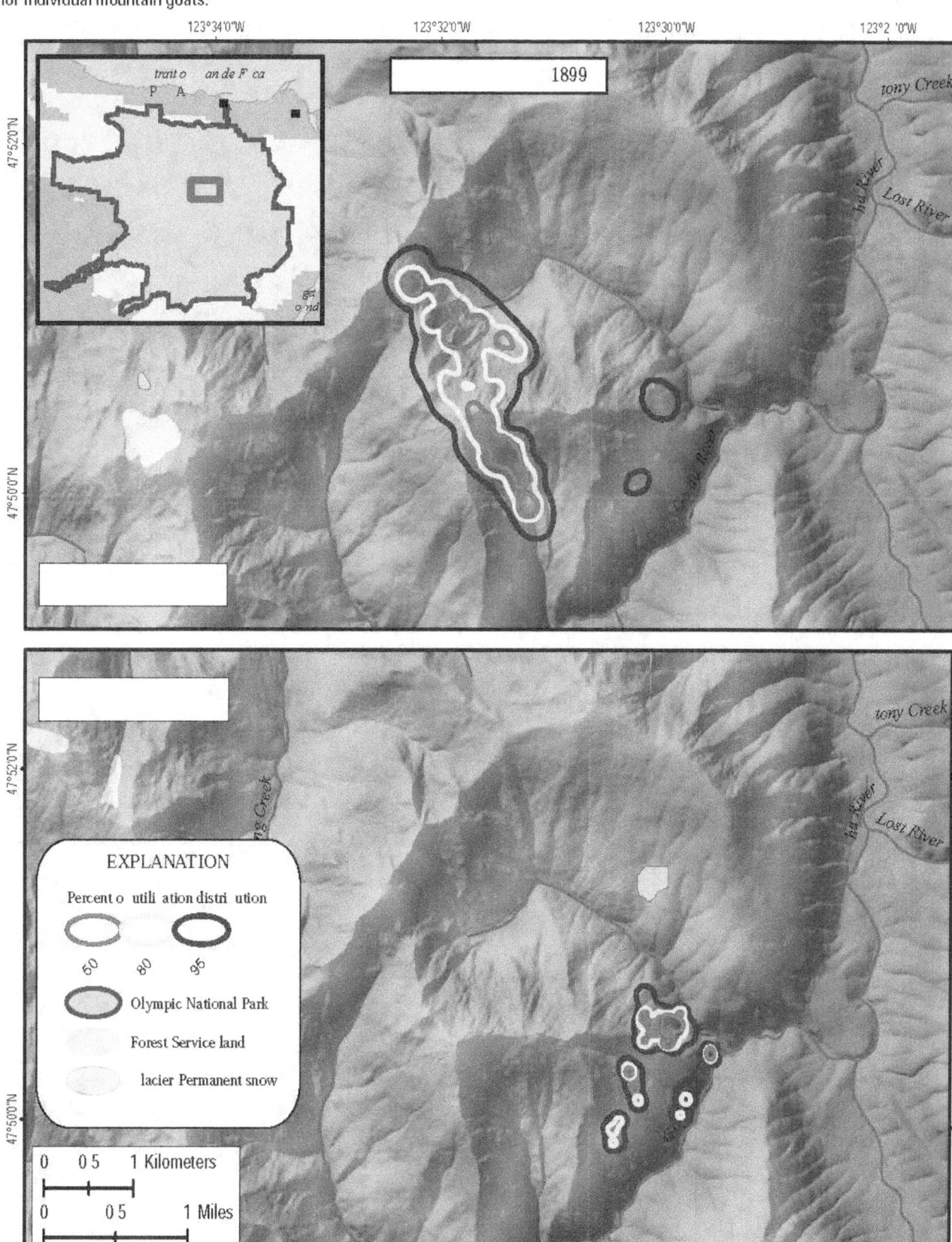

Appendix 3.   Maps showing seasonal distributions of selected GPS-collared mountain goats in Mount Rainier, North Cascades, and Olympic National Parks, Washington, 2003–07.—Continued. 95-, 80-, and 50-percent adaptive kernel utilization distributions are shown for individual mountain goats.

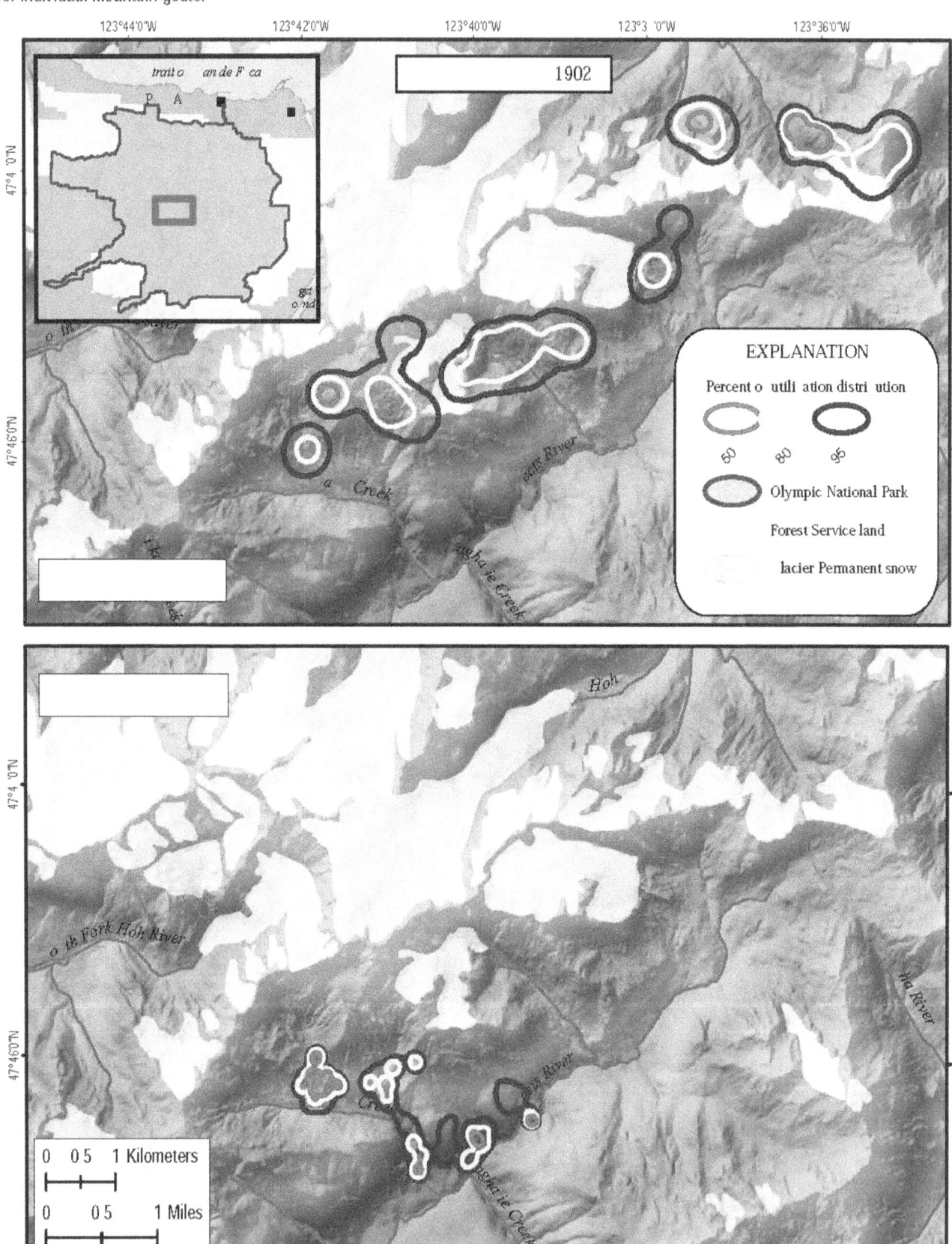

Appendix 4.   Maps showing polygons surveyed to provide sightability trials in the development of an aerial survey sightability model for mountain goats in Mount Rainier, North Cascades, and Olympic National Parks, Washington, 2006–07.

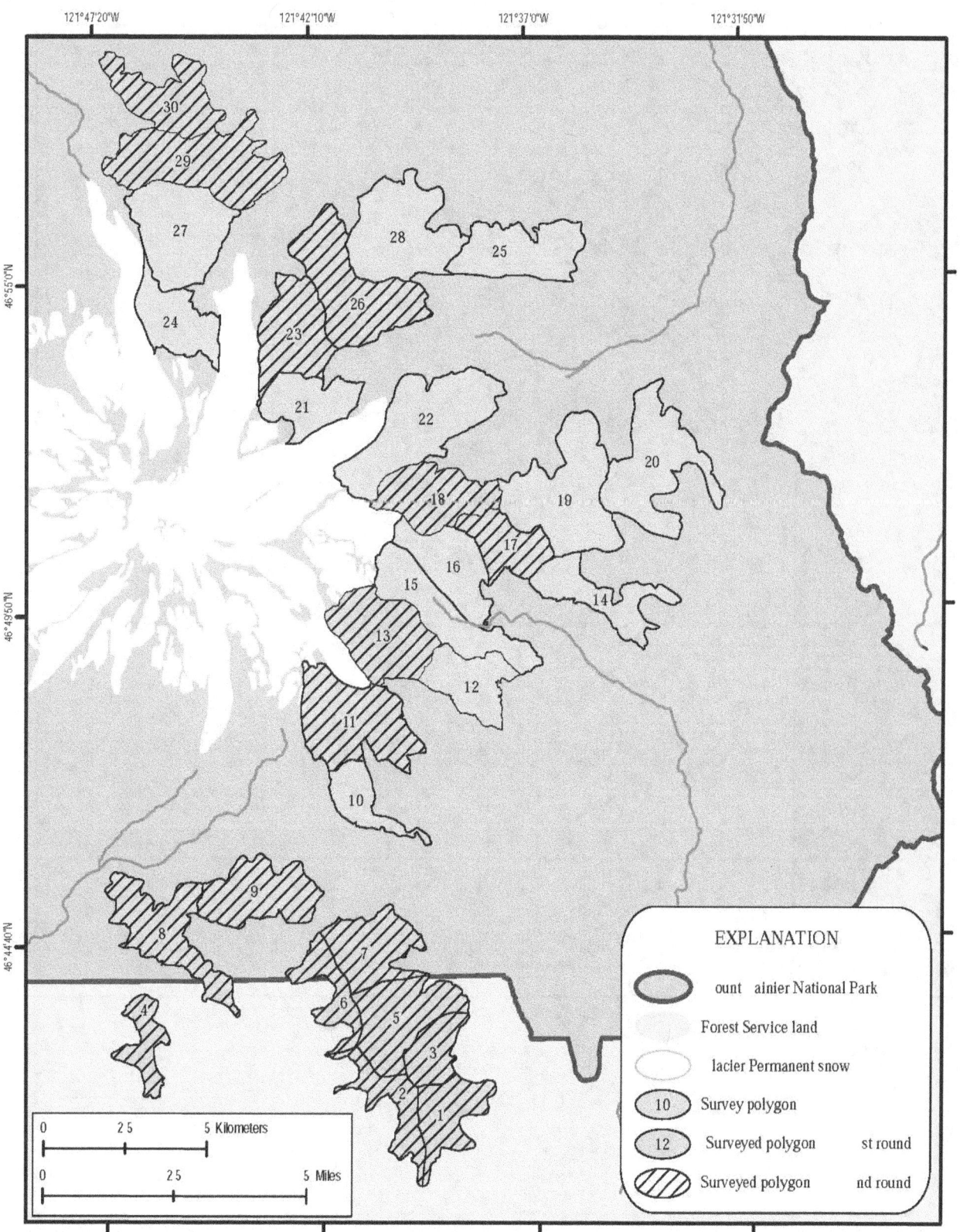

Appendix 4.   Maps showing polygons surveyed to provide sightability trials in the development of an aerial survey sightability model for mountain goats in Mount Rainier, North Cascades, and Olympic National Parks, Washington, 2006–07.—Continued

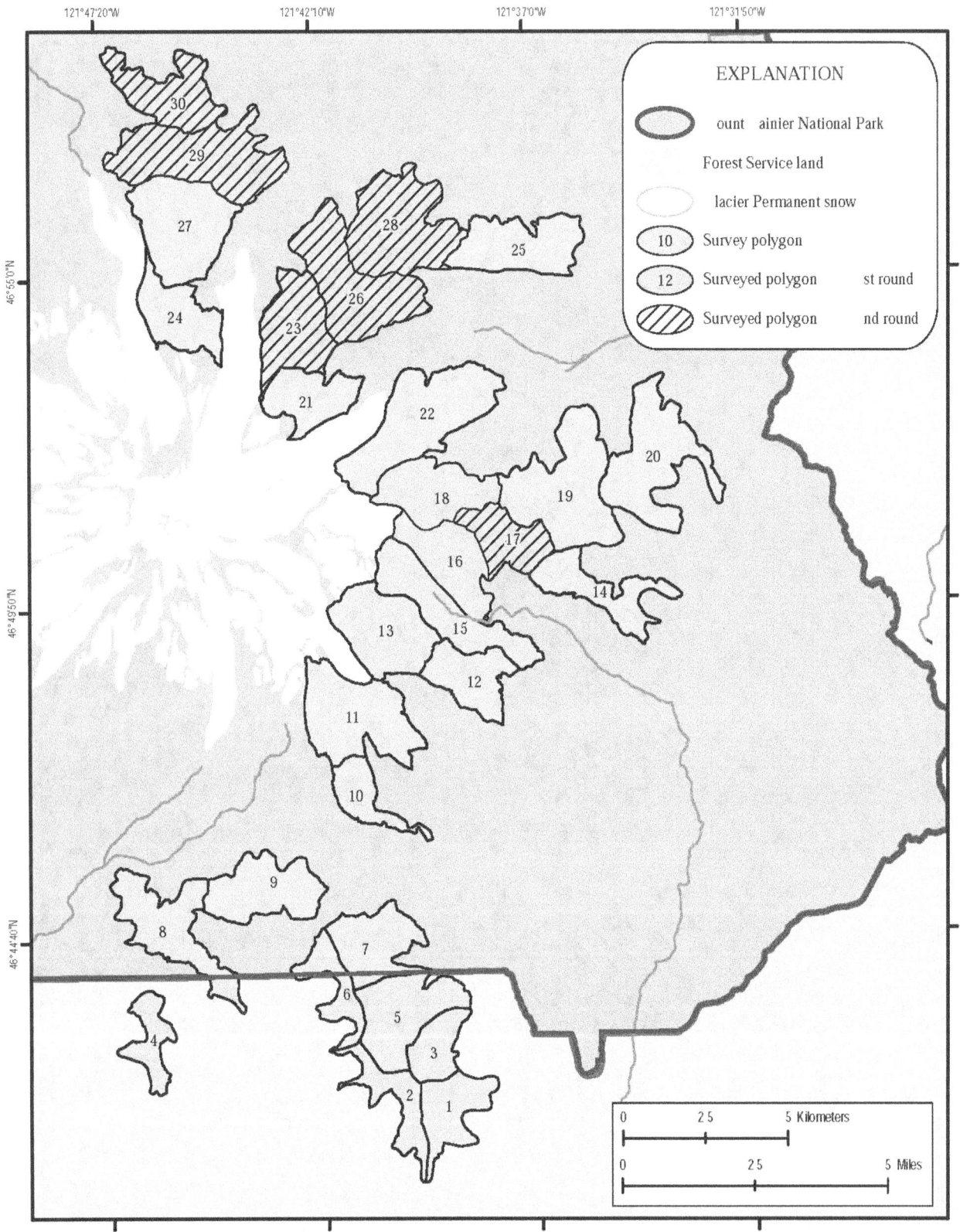

Appendix 4.   Maps showing polygons surveyed to provide sightability trials in the development of an aerial survey sightability model for mountain goats in Mount Rainier, North Cascades, and Olympic National Parks, Washington, 2006–07.—Continued

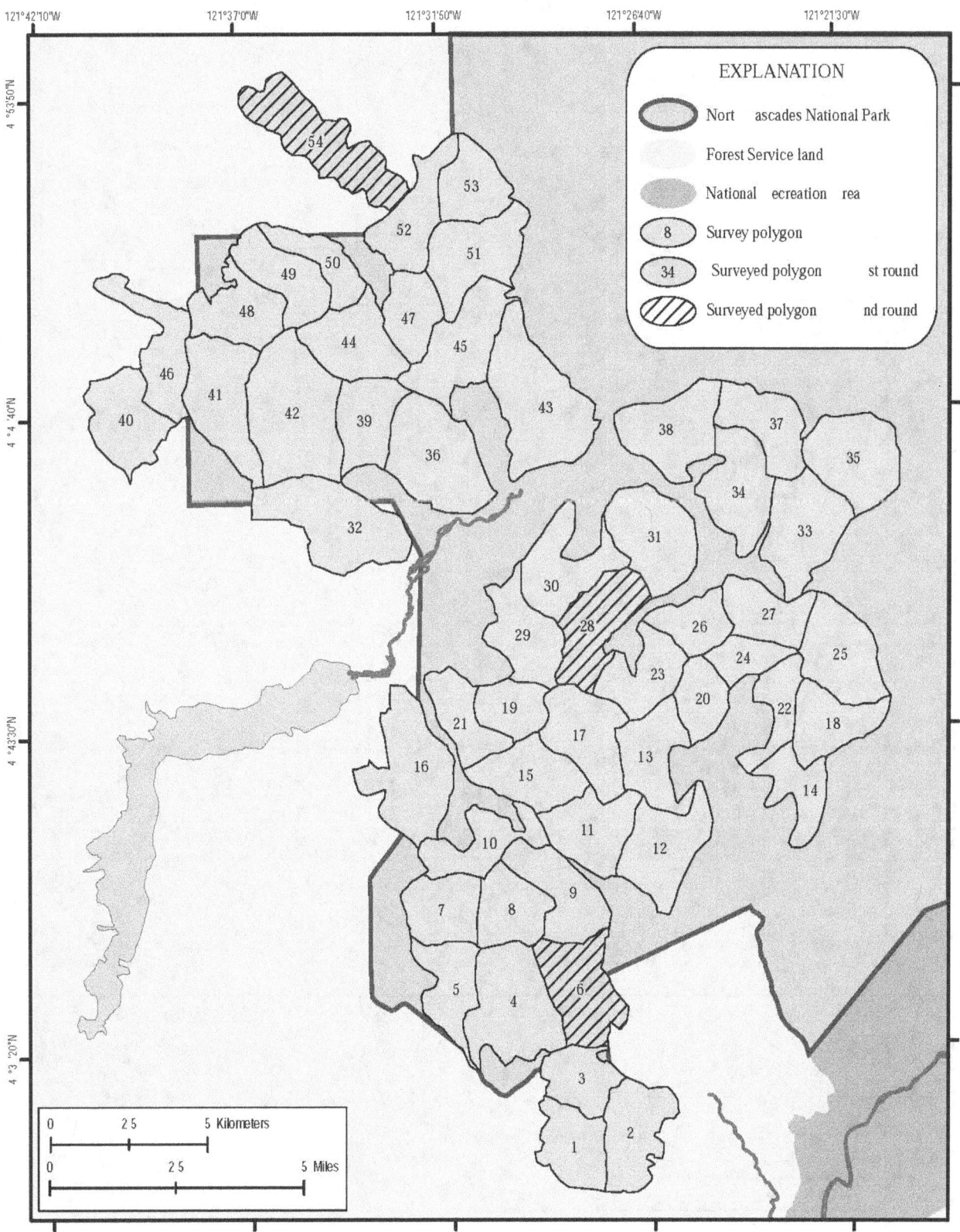

Appendix 4.   Maps showing polygons surveyed to provide sightability trials in the development of an aerial survey sightability model for mountain goats in Mount Rainier, North Cascades, and Olympic National Parks, Washington, 2006–07.—Continued

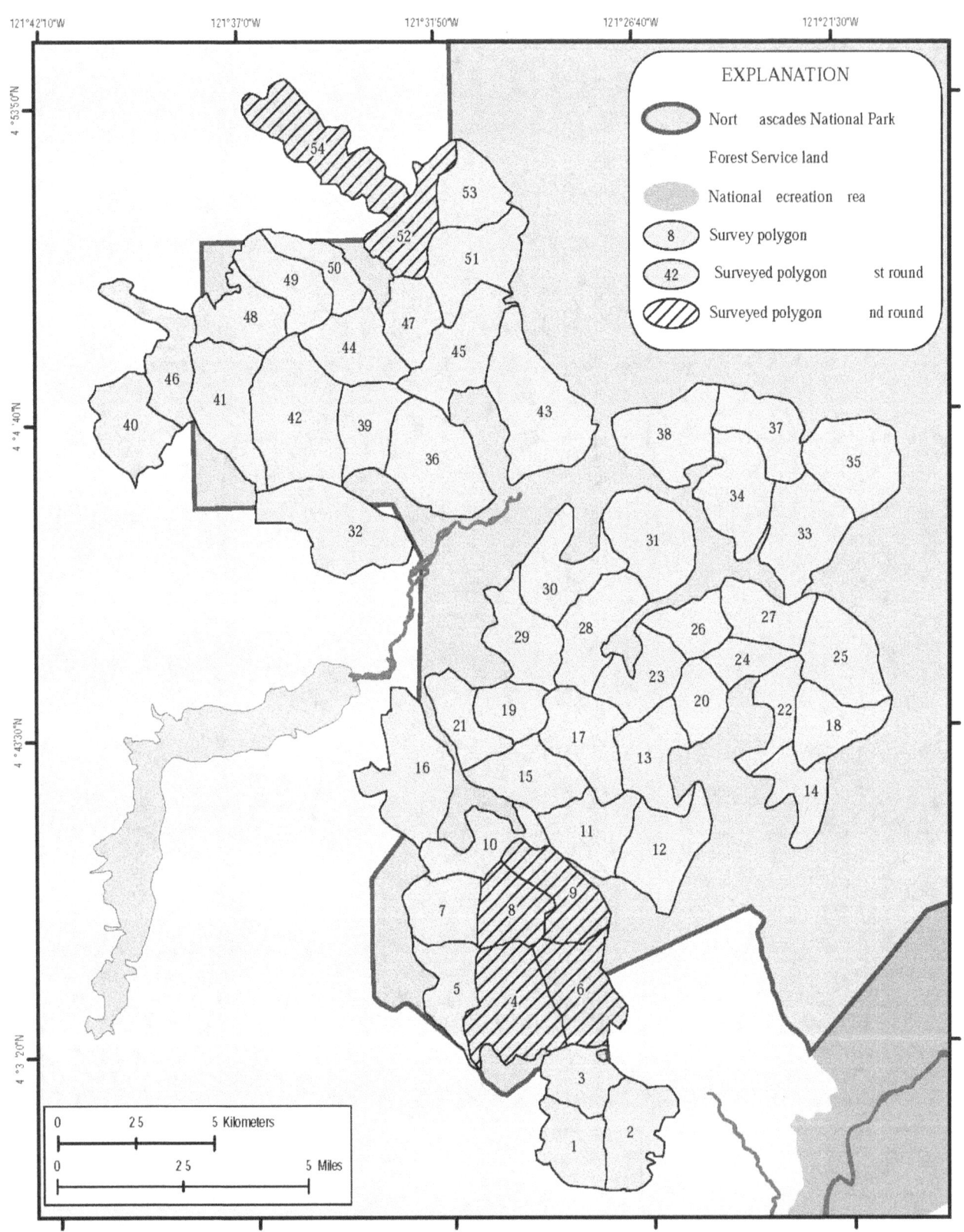

Appendix 4.   Maps showing polygons surveyed to provide sightability trials in the development of an aerial survey sightability model for mountain goats in Mount Rainier, North Cascades, and Olympic National Parks, Washington, 2006–07.—Continued

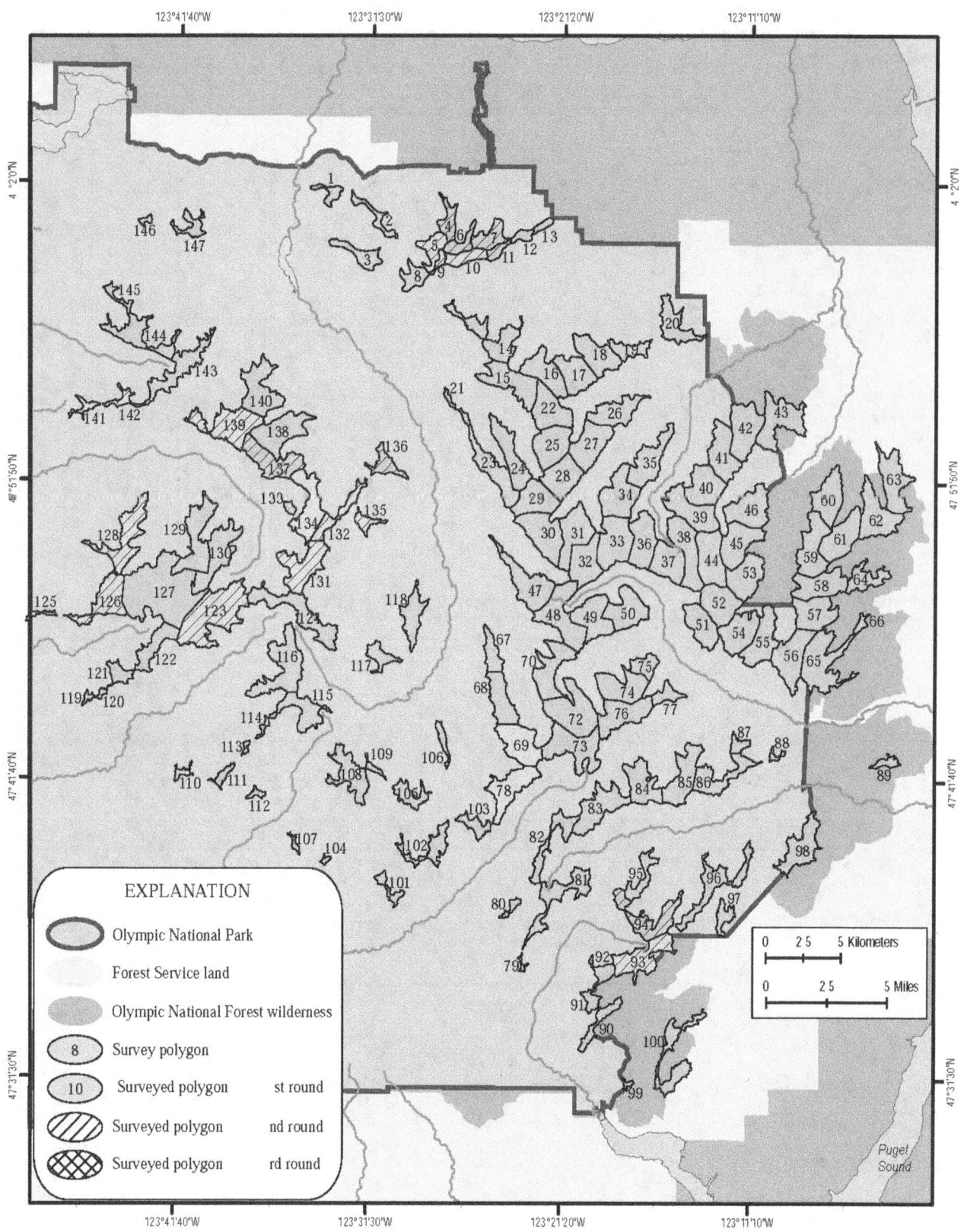

Appendix 4.   Maps showing polygons surveyed to provide sightability trials in the development of an aerial survey sightability model for mountain goats in Mount Rainier, North Cascades, and Olympic National Parks, Washington, 2006–07.—Continued

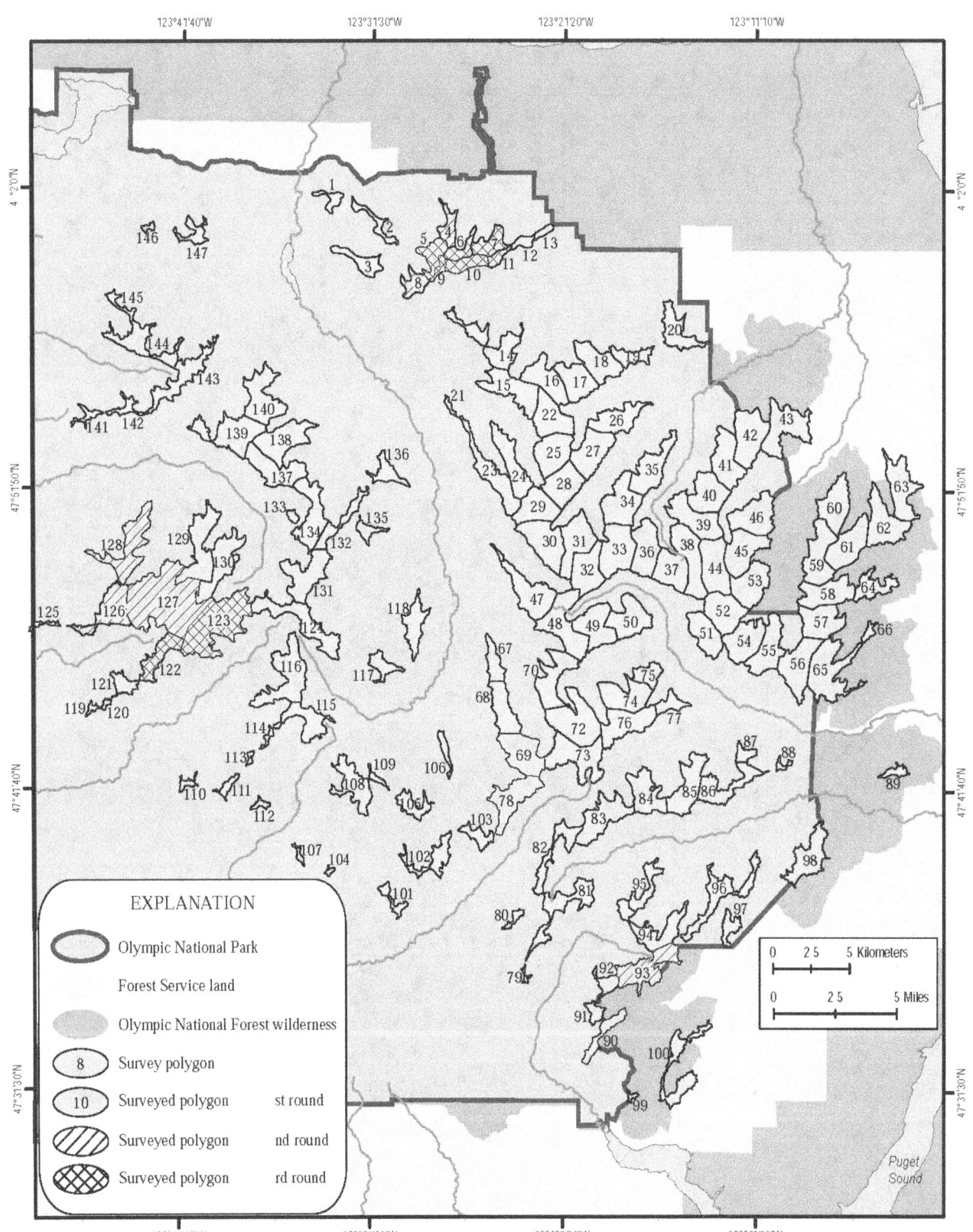

Appendix 5. Aerial survey characteristics and counts of mountain goats observed during aerial survey sightability trials in Mount Rainier, North Cascades, and Olympic National Parks, Washington, 2005–07.

[Time and temperature were recorded when beginning to survey the polygon or group of polygons. Complete?: Was the polygon (or group of polygons) surveyed entirely? For logistic reasons, not all surveys were complete in all polygons. °C, degrees Celsius; Temp, temperature, min, minute;, km^2, square kilometers; No., number; Unk, unknown]

| Date | Polygon | Survey characteristics | | | | | | Polygon | Counts | | | |
		Time	Temp (°C)	Complete?	Duration (min)	Area (km^2)	Intensity (min/ km^2)		No. of groups	Total	Kids	Unk
					Mount Rainier National Park							
07-17-06	12,13	6:27:00	9	no	22.8	6.4	3.6	12,13	4	24	5	0
07-17-06	18	6:56:41	10	yes	26.1	5.1	5.2	18	4	31	10	0
07-17-06	29	8:52:29	10	yes	36.8	8.3	4.5	29	3	6	0	0
07-17-06	30	9:30:00		yes	13.0	4.8	2.7	30	0	0	0	0
07-31-06	1	6:48:00	1	yes	8.0	3.8	2.1	1	0	0	0	0
07-31-06	2	7:56:00	1	yes	16.0	3.2	5.0	2	0	0	0	0
07-31-06	3	6:56:00	1	yes	7.0	2.6	2.7	3	0	0	0	0
07-31-06	4	8:16:00	1	yes	7.0	2.3	3.0	4	0	0	0	0
07-31-06	5	7:03:00	1	yes	12.0	5.8	2.1	5	0	0	0	0
07-31-06	6	7:42:00	5	yes	7.0	2.7	2.6	6	0	0	0	0
07-31-06	7	7:16:00	5	yes	21.0	4.7	4.5	7	4	14	4	0
07-31-06	8	9:37:00	7	yes	33.0	5.9	5.6	8	1	2	0	0
07-31-06	9	10:15:42	3	yes	20.0	5.3	3.8	9	0	0	0	0
07-31-06	11	10:48:18	4	yes	29.9	7.4	4.0	11	5	8	0	0
07-31-06	13	11:21:01	2	yes	12.0	6.2	1.9	13	3	26	4	0
07-31-06	18	13:49:00	5	yes	22.0	5.1	4.4	18	0	0	0	0
07-31-06	23	13:21:00	4	yes	20.0	5.3	3.8	23	2	4	1	0
07-31-06	26	12:50:48	4	yes	30.2	7.9	3.8	26	1	18	5	0
08-01-06	17	6:09:47	-1	yes	9.2	3.5	2.6	17	4	49	10	0
08-01-06	29	6:28:43	0	yes	26.3	8.3	3.2	29	0	0	0	0
08-01-06	30	6:56:05	-2	yes	13.9	4.8	2.9	30	0	0	0	0
07-11-07	16	7:07:26	19	yes	25.0	4.7	5.4	16	3	10	0	0
07-11-07	17	7:37:08	19	yes	15.0	3.5	4.3	17	3	5	0	0
07-11-07	18	7:56:41	19	yes	30.3	5.1	6.0	18	3	25	4	2
07-11-07	26	10:30:05	19	no	12.0	7.9	1.5	26	2	8	2	1
07-11-07	28	10:00:06	19	yes	27.8	7.8	3.6	28	0	0	0	0
07-11-07	29	5:21:29	20	yes	34.3	8.3	4.2	29	0	0	0	0
07-24-07	17	15:32:23	10	yes	16.1	3.5	4.6	17	4	49	11	0
07-24-07	23	16:30:54	6	yes	21.7	5.3	4.1	23	2	16	4	0
07-24-07	26	16:00:17	5	yes	29.0	7.9	3.7	26	4	27	2	0
07-25-07	28	8:34:53	9	yes	39.9	7.8	5.1	28	3	5	0	0
07-25-07	29	5:54:26	6	yes	30.4	8.3	3.7	29	4	5	0	0
07-25-07	30	6:27:38	8	yes	15.6	4.8	3.3	30	0	0	0	0
					North Cascade National Park							
07-18-06	3			no				3	1	1	0	0
07-18-06	4	11:24:50	10	yes	31.2	8.4	3.7	4	2	3	0	0
07-18-06	5			no				5	1	3	1	0
07-18-06	6	11:01:00	10	yes	22.0	6.4	3.4	6	0	0	0	0
07-18-06	9	9:43:00	8	yes	17.0	5.5	3.1	9	1	1	0	0
07-18-06	33	9:12:00	7	yes	23.0	7.0	3.3	33	2	2	0	0
07-18-06	34	8:46:00	7	yes	44.0	6.2	7.1	34	0	0	0	0
07-18-06	52	7:14:00	7	yes	19.0	5.2	3.7	52	2	2	0	0
07-18-06	54	6:31:20	7	no	41.7	8.1	5.2	54	8	18	4	0
08-02-06	6	6:13:10	6	yes	23.8	6.4	3.7	6	5	18	4	0
08-02-06	28	6:50:00	3	no	8.0	5.9	1.4	28	1	1	0	0
08-02-06	54	7:56:00	5	no	5.0	8.1	0.6	54	3	3	0	0

Appendix 5. Aerial survey characteristics and counts of mountain goats observed during aerial survey sightability trials in Mount Rainier, North Cascades, and Olympic National Parks, Washington, 2005–07.—Continued

[Time and temperature were recorded when beginning to survey the polygon or group of polygons. Complete?: Was the polygon (or group of polygons) surveyed entirely? For logistic reasons not all surveys were complete in all polygons. °C, degrees Celsius; Temp, temperature, min, minute;, km², square kilometers; No., number; Unk, unknown]

Date	Polygon	Survey characteristics						Polygon	Counts			
		Time	Temp (°C)	Complete?	Duration (min)	Area (km²)	Intensity (min/km²)		No. of groups	Total	Kids	Unk
North Cascade National Park—Continued												
07-12-07	6	8:03:28	20	yes	31.0	6.4	4.8	6	5	9	1	0
07-12-07	9	8:36:15	21	no	5.8	5.5	1.1	9	1	7	3	0
07-12-07	42	6:09:55	21	yes	31.0	10.6	2.9	42	9	24	7	0
07-12-07	54	5:31:40	21	yes	30.3	8.1	3.7	54	7	19	2	0
07-26-07	4	13:03:30	16	yes	38.5	8.4	4.6	4	3	14	2	0
07-26-07	6	10:59:30	10	yes	24.7	6.4	3.8	6	1	1	0	0
07-26-07	8	11:46:00	18	yes	21.0	4.5	4.7	8	3	3	0	0
07-26-07	9	11:25:20	10	yes	20.0	5.5	3.7	9	4	5	1	0
07-26-07	52	16:07:30	12	no	11.5	5.2	2.2	52	0	0	0	0
07-26-07	54	15:12:50	12	yes	53.2	8.1	6.6	54	6	11	1	0
Olympic National Park												
07-10-06	126	6:48:13	7	yes	26.9	2.8	9.5	126	16	25	3	0
07-10-06	128	6:13:11	7	yes	33.5	5.6	6.0	128	3	5	1	0
07-10-06	131	10:24:10	9	yes	29.7	4.6	6.4	131	1	3	1	0
07-10-06	132	10:53:53	9	yes	19.0	2.5	7.7	132	1	3	0	0
07-10-06	134	11:25:18	9	yes	18.1	5.1	3.6	134	0	0	0	0
07-10-06	135	11:13:45	9	yes	9.2	1.2	8.0	135	2	3	0	0
07-10-06	139	9:00:15	9	yes	28.5	5.5	5.2	139	4	14	4	0
07-10-06	141, [1]142	8:38:37	9	yes	19.7	1.8	10.8	141	0	0	0	0
								142	0	0	0	0
07-10-06	5, 9, [1]10	8:15:50	8	no	12.8	2.6	5.0	5	1	1	0	0
								9	1	3	1	0
								10	0	0	0	0
07-11-06	93	8:12:38	9	yes	41.4	5.1	8.1	93	13	22	3	0
07-11-06	123	6:13:30	8	yes	43.8	5.2	8.3	123	5	6	0	0
07-11-06	69, [1]78	9:00:15	9	yes	44.9	10.3	4.4	69	1	1	0	0
								78	27	55	11	1
07-24-06	123	7:31:23	18	yes	39.6	5.2	7.6	123	0	0	0	0
07-24-06	128	11:56:59	18	yes	23.5	5.6	4.2	128	3	5	1	0
07-24-06	142	9:27:40	18	yes	10.6	1.0	10.2	142	1	1	0	0
07-24-06	125, [1]126	11:20:09	18	yes	36.8	3.2	11.4	125	1	1	0	0
								126	8	12	1	0
07-24-06	137, [1]139	9:40:03	18	yes	51.0	10.4	4.9	137	1	7	3	0
								139	6	13	3	0
07-24-06	4, 5, 6, 7, 8, 9, 10, [1]11	5:53:40	18	yes	42.8	14.0	3.1	4	0	0	0	0
								5	1	1	0	0
								6	1	4	1	0
								7	2	2	0	0
								8	0	0	0	0
								9	0	0	0	0
								10	0	0	0	0
								11	0	0	0	0
07-26-06	131	9:17:23	18	yes	27.3	4.6	5.9	131	7	13	2	0
07-26-06	132	9:44:43	18	yes	15.3	2.5	6.2	132	1	1	0	0
07-26-06	135	10:00:00	18	yes	6.6	1.2	5.7	135	0	0	0	0
07-26-06	136	10:07:04	18	yes	6.8	2.0	3.4	136	0	0	0	0

Appendix 5.   Aerial survey characteristics and counts of mountain goats observed during aerial survey sightability trials in Mount Rainier, North Cascades, and Olympic National Parks, Washington, 2005–07.—Continued

[Time and temperature were recorded when beginning to survey the polygon or group of polygons. Complete?: Was the polygon (or group of polygons) surveyed entirely? For logistic reasons not all surveys were complete in all polygons. °C, degrees Celsius; Temp, temperature, min, minute;, km², square kilometers; No., number; Unk, unknown]

| Date | Polygon | Survey characteristics | | | | | | Polygon | Counts | | | |
		Time	Temp (°C)	Complete?	Duration (min)	Area (km²)	Intensity (min/km²)		No. of groups	Total	Kids	Unk
				Olympic National Park—Continued								
07-26-06	93, [1]94	7:00:43	12	yes	65.5	10.1	6.5	93	3	12	2	0
								94	2	4	1	0
07-09-07	90	8:43:46	13	yes	22.4	1.9	11.9	90	0	0	0	0
07-09-07	93	9:07:47	13	no	21.5	5.1	4.2	93	4	6	1	0
07-09-07	128	6:27:32	13	no	27.8	5.6	5.0	128	5	24	8	0
07-09-07	127N	5:41:53	13	yes	43.6	2.4	18.1	127N	8	14	3	0
07-09-07	5, 9, [1]10	7:43:24	12	no	18.8	2.8	6.7	5	1	2	0	0
								9	1	1	0	0
								10	0	0	0	0
07-10-07	123	5:48:38	12	no	1.8	5.2	0.3	123	0	0	0	0
07-10-07	69, [1]78	6:04:26	18	yes	77.8	10.3	7.6	69	5	7	1	0
								78	18	35	8	0
07-16-07	93	13:09:05	11	yes	44.4	5.1	8.7	93	3	19	6	0
07-16-07	123	11:05:29	11	yes	48.5	5.2	9.3	123	4	5	0	0
07-16-07	126	6:33:00	7	yes	40.5	2.8	14.4	126	10	15	3	0
07-16-07	128	7:15:42	7	yes	42.8	5.6	7.6	128	8	31	11	0
07-16-07	127N	10:34:52	11	yes	25.1	2.4	10.5	127N	4	13	3	0
07-16-07	4, 5, 6, 7, 8, 9, 10, [1]11	8:47:51	9	yes	49.1	14.0	3.5	4	0	0	0	0
								5	0	0	0	0
								6	1	1	0	0
								7	1	1	0	0
								8	0	0	0	0
								9	1	1	0	0
								10	0	0	0	0
								11	0	0	0	0
09-06-07	122E, [1]123W	13:16:20	9	no	22.4	2.8	7.9	122E	3	3	0	0
								123W	2	3	0	0
09-06-07	5, 6, 7, 9, 10, [1]11	11:54:00	10	no	42.6	7.5	5.7	5	0	0	0	0
								6	1	1	0	0
								7	2	2	0	0
								9	0	0	0	0
								10	0	0	0	0
								11	0	0	0	0

[1]These polygons were flown as a unit. Survey characteristics of individual polygons were not recorded.